POTTER

AND

CLAY

POTTER

AND

CLAY

Dorothy Cartwright

PETER WATTS

Publishing limited

ISBN 0 906025 69 9

Published by Peter Watts Publishing Ltd
Stag House, Gydynap Lane
Inchbrook
Woodchester, Gloucestershire

Design and layout: Peter Watts
Typesetting and artwork: Mopok Graphics, Glossop
Printed and Bound in Great Britain

This book is dedicated to my
dear late husband
John Geoffrey Garrett

CONTENTS

Line drawings and map by John Geoffrey Garrett

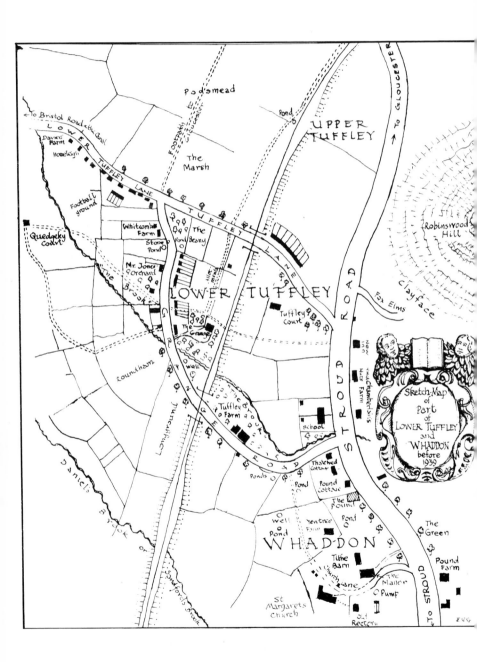

← To Bristol Road & the Canal

LOWER TUFFLEY LANE

Davies Farm

Homeleigh

Football ground

Quedgeley Court

Whitcombs Farm

Stone Pond

Mr Jones Orchard

The Brook

Roundham

TUFFLEY LANE

Pod's mead

Footpath

The Marsh

The Pond

The Beany

LOWER TUFFLEY

The Grange

well

Tuffley Farm

Pond

Pond

UPPER TUFFLEY

To Gloucester

STROUD ROAD

Robinswood Hill

Fox Elms

Clayface

New Chambers Hay Farm

Tuffley Court

school

Sketch-Map
of
Part
of
LOWER TUFFLEY
and
WHADDON
before
1939

Longford

Daniels Brook or

Schoolford's Brook

Ponds

Thatched Cottage

Pound Cottage

The Pound

Pound

Well Pond

Yewtree Farm

WHADDON

Tithe Barn

Church Lane

St Margarets Church

Old Rectory

The Manor

Pump

To Stroud

The Green

Pound Farm

E V G

ACKNOWLEDGEMENTS

I am indebted to many people for their help and encouragement while this book was being written, as well as to one who died many years ago—Benjamin John Herrin, first Headmaster of Whaddon Council School, for his unshakable belief that we are all 'greater than we know'.

For technical and historical help, my thanks are due to G. R. Hiatt, B.A., A.L.A., Divisional Librarian, Gloucester County Library, for information about the history of Tuffley and local place names, which gave me the inspiration to write to the best of my ability about my old village; to J. Haslem, Assistant Divisional Librarian, Gloucester County Library, for information and the names of books relevant to the Atkyns family; to the Very Reverend Gilbert Thurlow, Dean of Gloucester, for directing me to the whereabout of the archives of Tuffley; to D. J. H. Smith, B.A., County Archivist, Gloucester Records Office, for information and help concerning Tuffley Court, seat of the Atkyns family, who held the lease of the Manor of Tuffley, the Court and a Park, from the Dean and Chapter of Gloucester for some hundred years, until the middle of the seventeenth century; as well as checking the m.s. and giving his much appreciated advice. To Malcolm J. Watkins, Archaeology Assistant, City Museum and Art gallery, Gloucester, for his advice and research into the name of the brook which ran beside Grange Road; to John Hunter, B.Sc.(Econ.) M.A., Ph.D., Gloucestershire College of Education, for information about the Gloucester College of Domestic Science; to the Ministry of Agriculture, Fish and Food, Animal Health Department, Guildford, for information on modern methods of controlling foot and mouth disease; to Wynstones School, Whaddon, and Whaddon Junior School, for photographs and other items of interest.

To the daughters of the late Colonel Edward Stockley Sinnott, for their very careful account of the Colonel's life and family, and his quotation from Deuteronomy 29, v.11, 'Hewers of wood and drawers of water', besides much other and varied information, particularly about the ponds and footpaths, my thanks are due.

I am grateful to my sister, Naomi, and her husband, Herbert Wood, for sending me newspaper cuttings throughout the years and for reminding me of things which happened when we were young, as well as for details concerning Brother Michael; to my friend Simmy, who has also sent me newspaper cuttings about our village for more than 35 years, for asking her friend Marjorie Nash for stories of the early days of the newcomers to the village; to Lilian and Kenneth Cocks for stories about Lower Tuffley and for Lilian's help in pursuing the history of the Atkyns family; to Marjorie Nash for her help and interest and for recommending me to Elizabeth Vowles, who needs special thanks for her many letters recalling details which I would otherwise have forgotten and for giving me news of much which has occurred recently, of which I had no knowledge; to Patricia Wilson for notes and details concerning Robinswood Hill and the Brick and Tile Works; to Charles Jones of Whaddon, for his kindness in giving me the history of the two wells there. These people have helped continuously by their interest and enthusiasm.

I am grateful to Gertrude Winter for her beautiful typescript, great interest and occasional correction in matters of phraseology; with special thanks to Diana St. John for editorial help.

Finally, my thanks and appreciation to my dear husband, John Geoffrey, who visited distant Libraries for me when our own Reference Library was out of commission owing to a fire and I was unable to travel, for his constant encouragement and interest, and for the drawings and the map of Lower Tuffley as I remember it.

Thank you all for the book which has resulted.

Should any readers find discrepancies, I beg them to remember the time which has elapsed between the actual event and its recording.

D.C

Chapter One   Our Village

The sun was setting behind the fields west of our village; the birds were silent and the air was calm and still, filled with the scent of summer flowers. People talked quietly over their garden hedges or sat on their benches, glad of a quiet time before supper after the day's toil.

Suddenly the peace was shattered, as from a house a few doors away a raucous voice was heard. An old lady was trying to help a deaf old man to fill in his census form: 'Old man, whur wuss you barned?' she shouted. There was silence for a time while the old man pondered. 'Oi don't know as oi wuss barned anywhur' he said hesitantly. He was puzzled by the question and hardly knew what to answer. He had been born a very long time ago.

Mother told us this story many times when we were young, to illustrate how difficult it was for people who were unable to read or write to understand and deal with forms. The people of our village, Lower Tuffley, were not in tune with the lovely quiet evening. Old people, particularly, resented giving answers to what they considered their own private business and telling where they had been born was, to them, very private. Many of them became worried to distraction, and the younger ones, who were able to read and write, were called in to help. The old man who was so troubled had been born locally, but like so many of us who were born much later than he, did not think of our village as being 'anywhur'.

Pondering on this, I was inclined to agree with him. Our village consisted of four farms of varying sizes, one large house and, perhaps, fifty medium-sized brick houses. These had all been built of good red bricks made from the quarry at Robinswood Hill, during the nineteenth and early twentieth centuries. There were also two sixteenth or seventeenth century thatched cottages. The farms varied in age, parts of Tuffley Farm, Whitcombe Farm and the old Tuffley Court—a long, low, timbered building—dated back to the sixteenth or seventeenth century. There was one public house—the New Inn.

We had two wild, winding lanes, each of which joined the Gloucester to Stroud road. They met, Grange Road making a T junction with Tuffley Lane, which continued to the Gloucester to Bristol road. Along the loop formed by these two lanes and the Stroud road, lay short rows of houses, on one side of the lane only. Nowhere, until 1940, were there rows of houses on both sides of the roads.

Except for Tuffley farm, there were no dwellings between the Council School, at the Stroud road end of Grange Road, and the Grange, a distance of three-quarters of a mile. Fields stretched back from the lanes and the Stroud

Tuffley Farm in the 1920s. Mr F. Cartwright stands in the milk float whilst Saul Savage, the farm owner, is to the rear, hatted with a boater.

Grange Villa, alias Tuffley Dairy, photographed during the Second World War before the road was widened. The large 'B', painted onto the front facing wall, indicated that there was a bucket of water, and one of sand, always available in case of fire.

road as far as the eye could see, with only scattered houses and the tower of Whaddon Church breaking the green landscape.

The Grange was a large house with spacious grounds — gardens, lawns and orchards; several of the smaller houses had obviously been built for the people who served it. The lodge, for the gardener, was next to ours — Grange Villa — which had been built with white stone floors to serve as a dairy. We, also, had an orchard and a paddock for stock. Originally, other workers at the Grange used to live in Grange Cottages, but by the early part of the present century the serving system was breaking down and, apart from Grange Villa and the Lodge, the home of the coachman/gardener, which still belonged to the Grange, and other houses were inhabited by families who worked either for themselves or for different employers. There were a few tied cottages belonging to local farmers, but the majority, then, were owned by landlords who let them and used the rents for income.

Until World War II, there were always three servants at the Grange, and the daughters of Colonel Sinnott, who lived there, were educated at home before going to the High School.

We had no church within Lower Tuffley, so technically it rated as a hamlet. Our parish was divided between Tuffley itself (which had always been considered a separate district), where the small church of St. Barnabas stood, and Whaddon, where St. Margaret's church, built in the thirteenth century with foundations possibly a thousand years old, still stands. The Upper Tuffley part of the district grew rapidly and St. Barnabas was enlarged, first by a temporary wooden building and, later, by the beautiful modern church on its mound facing the little church. Lower Tuffley, with the exception of a few houses built to fill gaps, remained unchanged until the late 1930s.

All our houses were surrounded by gardens. There were few lawns, because we all relied heavily on what we grew or reared; vegetables, fruit, chickens, ducks and pigs. These made us a community providing a great deal of the food we needed; one large field, where the soil was good, was turned into allotments after the end of World War I. We did not live in an affluent society, but neither were we short of life's necessities. To most people, all this seemed very ordinary and we just accepted our village for what it appeared to be, a rambling community of no special importance, surrounded by beautiful country and encircled by the Cotswold hills in the distance. It has been described as 'compassing four miles'.

Only when I began to collect memories of Lower Tuffley did thoughts about its origin arise. Was there once someone named Tuffley who lived here? I wrote to Gloucester County Library for information and suddenly, after many years of taking our village for granted, my complacency was shattered. Mr G. R. Hiatt, the Divisional Librarian, sent me photocopies of pages referring to Tuffley taken from Robert Atkyns' The Ancient and Present State of Gloucestershire, Pt. 1, and A. H. Smith's Place names of Gloucestershire, Pt.2. These two extracts set out facts about Tuffley which led to months of exciting and satisfying discoveries.

Tuffley was named in the Domesday Book and changed during the centuries after 1086 from Tuffelege through many spellings to Tuffley. Mr Smith, the County Archivist, considers that the meaning of the name was 'Tuffa's glade' or 'clearing', and supports an older theory that 'Tuffa' was a later name for 'Tunfrid', which would make the settlement Old English rather than Old Norse. How old was our village? No one really knows, but it certainly began in prehistory. What were Tuffa and his people like? What sort of lives did they lead? Where exactly did he choose to settle with his family and friends? Did he make the clearing or was it already there? These are fascinating things for conjecture, but the whole valley is filled with remnants of a prehistoric civilisation, and Tuffley and Lower Tuffley, which covered four miles, had, even in the early part of this century, still traces of ancient habitation. Names, customs, associations, still link our village with early development.

This knowledge brought great excitement and a determination to do justice as far as I possibly could to so ancient an heritage. There was real joy in knowing that our community had developed slowly through possibly five or seven thousand years.

Old tracks criss-crossed the valleys which lie at the feet of the Cotswolds. They were the means of communication and commerce which increased as they became established. Pasture and arable land lay beside the tracks and stones of varying sizes marked (and some still do mark) the positions of these first roads.

Salt was one of the useful commodities carried along the tracks and it must have been taken through Tuffa's Ley from the salt flats along the Severn. Whitcombe Farm which stood in Grange Road must have been a trading post for salt (Whit O.E. for salt, combe for a little wooded hollow). It would probably have been carried through Whitminster (Salt Abbey or Priory). The monks who lived there at the dawning of Christianity would have been able to earn a good living by collecting salt and bartering it with the men who travelled the tracks, and they in turn would barter it at the trading posts which grew gradually for cloth or some other necessity of life.

The water in and around Stroud, some eight miles away, has been prized for countless years for its purity, and cloth dyed there took on deep clear tones. Scarlet in particular was dyed in Stroud for hundreds of years. The cloth would have been taken to the West via Brookthorpe and Whaddon and this track continued as far as Hereford. Tuffley was on the same route.

St. Peter's Abbey, (now Gloucester Cathedral), existed in 681AD and was supplied by the Sheephouse, (now Tuffley Avenue) with wool and mutton from the 11th century until the Dissolution.

Through the ancient tracks, and later along the Roman roads, trade expanded from this country to the Continent and the countries around our shores. Spices and silks from the East came to this country to be bartered or bought by people who were becoming wealthy. Robinswood Hill, whose steep slopes are climbed by the houses of Upper Tuffley, is a beacon hill, as are many of the high points on the Cotswolds. On these, from time immemorial, fires have been lit to convey warnings or other messages. They played an important part in spreading news, which travelled fast even in the days before any writing took place. Still today, in the twentieth century, the beacons blaze in a ring round the Cotswolds to tell of great events which are taking place.

During World War II, Gloucester and all the Cotswold towns knew that if England were invaded, the beacons would signal their warning.

Further evidence of the continuous occupation of Tuffley was provided by some very old wells and a number of coins dating back to Roman times which were discovered when, early in the present century, some new houses were built at the junction of Grange Road and Tuffley Lane. One of these was named 'Owels', thus commemorating these ancient wells.

Mr G. R. Hiatt, Divisional Librarian of Gloucester, helped me greatly by supplying copies of references to Tuffley, which, throughout early centuries, was frequently mentioned in Gloucester records. The fullest early account is in Robert Atkyns' book, *The Ancient and Present State of Gloucestershire*, first published about 1712. He described Tuffley as 'lying in the parish of St. Mary de Lode in the City of Gloucester, and in the Hundred of King's Barton, one mile and a half South East of Gloucester'. He states that the Church of St. Peter (now the Cathedral) held Tuffley in Dudstones Hundred in the Manor of Bertune, in the reign of King Edward the Confessor. Atkyns goes on to say, 'It had been alienated from the Church of Gloster, but was again recovered to them by Bishop Osborne of Exeter, when Serlo was Abbot. It continued in the Abbey of Gloster until the dissolution and was granted to the Dean and Chapter'. This was written in 1672.

Friends living near Gloucester, Lilian Cocks and Elizabeth Vowles, have given much valuable information, which has helped to piece together the story of the village and the Atkyns family, and I am greatly indebted to them, and also to my husband for doing much research at a time when I was unable to travel to get data.

F. A. Hyatt writes of an early Richard Atkyns (a member of an old Gloucestershire family), who died in 1529. In his account of Gloucester he says 'Bells were cast in Gloucester by Richard Atkyns', giving the date of his death as above. This is to old Tuffleyites most interesting. Great Peter, the largest bell in England, hangs in Gloucester Cathedral. It is not known who cast the bell. Its inscription reads, 'The Convent had me cast in the name of Peter'. Great Peter, weighing three tons, was cast towards the end of the fifteenth century in a foundry which would not have been too far away because of the size of the bell. The foundry at Gloucester was large and capable of doing the work and at its head was Richard Atkyns, whose family later came to live in Tuffley.

David Atkyns, the first of the Atkyns family to live in Tuffley Court, came from Chepstow at the end of his life and died in 1552. The family leased the house, a park and estate, from the Dean and Chapter of Gloucester Cathedral and were there for about a hundred years. I was enable to establish this with the help of Mr D. H. Smith, B.A., County Archivist, and it gave me great joy. It was like finding buried treasure.

Several members of the family were barons of the Exchequer and two were Chief Barons. Almost all of them were interested in the Law, and spent time at Lincoln's Inn Fields. One, Colonel Richard Atkyns, who lived from 1615 to 1677, was famous for his great loyalty to Charles I during the Civil War. Although Gloucester (in charge of Colonel Edward Massey, aged 23) was Parliamentarian, like much of the surrounding countryside, Richard raised a troup of 140 horse and fought on the side of the King. Colonel Richard Atkyns' life was a chequered one. He was educated at home by two clerks and then

14

went to the (Free) Crypt School in Gloucester. At fourteen he went to Balliol College, Oxford, where he studied for two years, but failed to get a degree. Then, like other male members of his family, he went to Lincoln's Inn. Not liking the Law, he left there and travelled abroad with the only son of Lord Arundel of Wardour.

While Richard was a Protestant, he was influenced towards the Roman Catholic Church by the English College in Paris. After three years travelling, on the death of Arundel he returned to England and became interested in country matters. He also helped to set up a printing press at Oxford. The first edition of one of his pamphlets, entitled *'The Original and Growth of Printing'*, is in the British Museum. This was reprinted in 1664.

On the death of his father in 1636, he succeeded to the family estate, with an income of £800 per annum.

The Civil War broke out in 1642 and in that year Colonel Richard raised his troop of horse to ride for the King. This he did at his own expense. He was present at many local skirmishes as well as some of the main battles. These included a skirmish with Sir William Waller at Littledean; he was also at Roundway Down, Reading, Bath, Bristol and at the raising of the siege of Gloucester. After the war, he was heavily punished for his loyalty to the King (R. Atkyns says Colonel Richard Atkyns suffered much by his loyalty to King Charles I). His father was another Richard Atkyns of Tuffley, who lived at Tuffley Court. Colonel Atkyns was the last of his family to live there, for his home and lands were sequestrated and he had to pay £140 compensation.

In 1640, he had married Martha, Lady Acheson, who was the possessor of a considerable fortune. The marriage was not a happy one and he died in 1677 without leaving an heir. Colonel Atkyns spent three years of his life in the Marshalsea prison as a debtor. It was said that his wife had many extravagances.

During the Civil War, he would probably have visited Charles, whose headquarters was at Matson House, about three miles distant. The two young princes, Charles and James (each to become King in their turn, Charles II and James II), were at Matson with their father. They were locked in one of the rooms for safety, and as they were given nothing to do, they occupied themselves by carving their names in the panelling and cutting notches in the stone windowsills.

Matson House is at the present time a school and the children there, especially those who work in the same room as the young princes did, enjoy their history and are happy to learn about the association of the King and his sons with Gloucester.

Charles did not succeed in taking the City, the Parliamentarians arrived just in time to prevent it. One of the beacons, the one near Wainloads Hill, was lit to tell the people of Gloucester that help was coming, though the actual arrival of the Parliamentarian soldiers was about ten days later. Colonel Richard was pardoned in 1646, after the war had ended, though he never returned to Tuffley. The last part of his life was spent at Sapperton, which had been purchased by Baron Atkyns. After the restoration of the monarchy, he was made Deputy Lieutenant of Gloucester, a Justice of the Peace, and a Militia officer. Died without issue in 1677 and buried at St. George the Martyr, Southwark.

Because of the sequenstration, no building was allowed to take place on the fields between Lower Tuffley and the outskirts of Gloucester; no trees were allowed to stand in the fields, nothing which could jeopardize Gloucester again. Although building land was desperately needed, no building occurred until late in the 1930s.

Robert Atkyns, the author, says that in 1677 there were twenty-six houses and about one hundred and ten inhabitants in the whole of Tuffley; three of these were freeholders. The two thatched cottages were timbered buildings with Tudor brick filling, and must have been the remnant of the twenty-six which Tuffley possessed in Robert Atkyns' day. They were both pulled down in the first half of this century. The Court itself survived until 1942, though it has since been reduced to the size of a small house.

For many years it was an orphanage for boys, who, with the help of their foster parents ran the house and farm, learning to support themselves from an early age. They learned through experience. One of their daily jobs was to peel potatoes. If they failed to peel them, nothing was said, but no potatoes appeared on the dinner table! Their bread was weighed out to six ounces each day per boy. They helped to run the farm and among other crops, they often grew a large acreage of sugar beet. The boys helped with weeding and hoeing. In days when sugar was badly needed, the crop at Tuffley Court played its part. There was as much freedom as possible, and on Sundays the boys were allowed to visit local families, two at a time, for tea. Lilian Cock's family had two each week.

Many of the boys did well and there were schemes organised by interested people to help them. One such provided for passage and education, as well as employment later, for two boys to go to Canada. One of the boys who lived at the Court, Donald Hall, bought a railway carriage and a small piece of land. He fitted the carriage up as a shoe repairing shop and, in addition, provided the boots for the Lower Tuffley football team. Everyone in the village took their repairs to Donald, who executed his work well and at a moderate price. Our village could well have been self-supporting, if necessary.

Books containing information on the Atkyns family include:-

Atkyns, Sir. R. *The ancient and present state of Glostershire*, 1712 (2nd ed. 1768, reprinted 1976).

Austin, R. Sir Robert Atkyns the younger, *Transactions of the Bristol and Gloucestershire Archaeological Society*, ix, 1938.

Some account of Sir Robert Atkyns the younger and other members of the Atkyns family, *Transactions of the Bristol and Gloucestershire Archaeological Society*, XXXV, 1912.

Dictionary of National Biography, Vol. 2, 1885.

Hyett, F. A. *Gloucester in national history*, 1924.

Malcolm, J. P. *Lives of the topographers and antiquaries*, 1815 (includes Sir Robert Atkyns).

Notes and Queries (1910-12, Series II, ii, 474-5; v,448; vi, 137-9, 392. (Sir Robert Atkyns, Atkyns family).

Smith, A. H. *Place Names in Gloucestershire*. Pt.2, 1964.

Smith, B. Sir Robert Atkyns, in, *English Country Historians*, J. Simmons, ed., 1978.

Vindication of Richard Atkyns esquire. As also a relation of several passages in the western-war wherein he was concern'd, 1669.

Young, P. ed. *The Civil War: Richard Atkyns*, Military Memories Series, 1967.

Chapter Two   World War One

I was almost two years old when World War I broke out, so did not fully realise what war meant, but rather grew older accepting the state of things as they were, feeling secure at home.

Our mother's and father's bedroom was next door to my sister's and my room and we listened—while they thought we were asleep—to them discussing my father's being called into the forces.

We had our own dairy business, so, strictly speaking, he need not have gone, but like all able-bodied men he felt impelled to do 'his bit'. Mother tried to dissuade him: 'But you wouldn't be called up, you have a one-man business', she said repeatedly. Dad was adamant. He sold his business to Tuffley Farm and joined up. All the men of our village and its neighbouring village, Whaddon, joined up, not waiting to be called. For most it was their first experience of leaving their roots and separating from each other. Some families had several members, each in his own home. Few were able to serve in the same camp together.

My father had the sight of only one eye; he was blinded while a boy when he and his friends were playing with a waggoner's whip, making it crack. The knot caught him in his left eye and he never had sight in it again. He was not allowed to go on active service abroad for this reason and, although he hated being held back, was probably much more fortunate than many of our friends. Some fought at Mons and Ypres and either did not return or came home to England badly wounded.

Ernie Haines was one of those who were disabled and sent back to 'Blighty'. He and his family lived in a cottage opposite to us. There were several brothers and they all joined the forces. One of them died long after the end of the war from the effects of gas and wounds. Ernie was badly wounded (from France he was returned to Brighton General Hospital, where he stayed under treatment for many months) and like many others he had to go to hospital from time to time to have pieces of shrapnel removed from his body. Later, when he recovered, he was able to live an active life again.

While in hospital, Ernie fell in love with his nurse, Ethel, and later brought her home to Lower Tuffley as a bride. She had lived in London and badly missed the big city all her life. Like many families, hers had been a close and caring group, but the coming of war separated all of them, and only occasionally did members come to visit Ethel and Ernie. They were a devoted couple and when Ernie was free from work, they were rarely apart; we often saw them walking their dogs in the evenings.

Lower Tuffley lost several of its men. There was no picking and choosing. Victims came from the Manor at Whaddon, from farms, and cottages—every sort of home knew its loss either in the village or among relatives elsewhere. For three or four years, most homes were without the man of the house; in some cases both father and son were called up. Those who were left, the sick, the old, those few who were indispensable, like the farmers and the women, all found that life had changed completely.

We were very small then, and Ernie's wife, Ethel, was very different from our neighbours. We were in awe of her for a long time. She wore smart clothes, spoke with a different accent from ours, and because she had been a nurse, was often needed in the village. She was capable and had a fund of quiet wisdom. She and Ernie loved children and the village youngsters, who had known the big kindly man since they were tiny, called him either 'Uncle Ernie' or 'Ernie', but his dear wife was always known as 'Mrs Haines'. Thus it was for us until the day we moved away from Lower Tuffley and until the time this loving couple grew old and death separated them from the village.

Mrs Haines became a wonderful friend to local children who gradually developed the habit of going to her to discuss their troubles. She always listened kindly, her head on one side, and at the end of the narrative would give her considered opinion, sympathy and, if she could, good advice. We went away bathed and bandaged if we had fallen and grazed ourselves, comforted if we had quarrelled or been hurt mentally. Our village was a friendly community and we had no dearer friends than Ernie and Mrs Haines.

Our own mother was beautiful when she and Dad first came to Lower Tuffley. She was tall, with very black hair, done in a 'bun-on-top'. She, too, was smartly dressed at first, but, as with everyone else who came to live there, this lasted just until her town clothes wore out. Then country clothes and serviceable shoes were bought as replacements. Our smallholding became mother's responsibility. The life she led demanded stout shoes and boots as barriers against the mud in wet weather and snow in winter. I remember she had some pattens which, when the mud was very bad, she strapped on under her shoes. They were circular metal frames, built up about two inches and they lifted skirts and shoes out of the mud, although they must have been difficult and rather unsafe to walk on. Mother wore clogs when feeding the stock in bad weather — rubber gum boots had not been invented then. The coming of war, which forced women to do all sorts of work previously done by men, must have been a contributing factor in shortening skirts. Ground length skirts (which were always braided at the hem, because they wore out so quickly) were taken up gradually, until they were mid-calf length and women moved more freely than they had done before.

My sister was a year younger and my brother two years younger than I and both were born during the war, so, like the rest of the village children, we grew up accepting the fact that fathers came home only occasionally. Some had to get used to the idea that Daddy would never come home again, while others grew up early, doing the work that an ailing parent would, perhaps, never be able to do again. One of my brother's friends was an example of this. Alban's father lost his health and after he returned home was ill for the rest of his life. Alban, although very young, quickly learned the skills of tending a garden and he acquired specialised arts as well, one of which was grafting and budding trees. His grafts always grew and the rose trees in the Cole's garden were a mass of huge blooms. He played jokes on many people, grafting scions of different varieties of fruit on to the same tree, budding rose stocks with more than one kind of rose bud. People always had good value from the new fruit or roses, so they forgave Alban his jokes.

My father carried despatches, and when he came to Gloucester, he visited home, if he could, for a few hours. Mother worried a great deal in case he got into trouble. He came chiefly to see if she needed help and give advice.

One of the things he did at this time was to build us a driveway of our own. He used leave to accomplish it. The descent from our house to the road was steep, and having no driveway of our own had meant sharing the drive of the house next door or having to go up and down many steps with a pram. This was inconvenient for all concerned, so the driveway when it came was very welcome.

Nothing was ever to be the same after the war years. With the men away, women had to take over the work usually done by them. Gardening, poultry and pig keeping, farm work, work in the factories, became the way of life for people who had never worked outside a house previously. We had no water laid on, so it had to be drawn from the wells; lavatory buckets had to be emptied. Jobs, clean and dirty alike, came to be an accepted part of life. The war, more than any other factor, gave women freedom. They had to have a vote—men realised that if women downed tools now, they might as well give in at once. Many jobs that they undertook because they had to, have remained in the hands of women, who found they liked doing them.

A great many younger women went to work in the munitions factory. Ironically, the quickest way to reach it was by crossing the beautiful meadows which lay between Tuffley and Quedgeley. The factory worked day and night shifts and ammunition of one sort or another was being manufactured there continuously.

The place had a morbid fascination for all the children, and, if the red flag was not flying to show that it was dangerous, we wandered over the fields, going as near as possible, trying to see what was going on. We couldn't, of course. At times we heard explosions, when ammunition, judged to be faulty, was detonated. We waited just long enough for the red flag to be pulled down and then set out and searched the fields for finds. We found spent bullets and pieces of plaid silk, which had wrapped the explosive inside the shells. This was usually badly burnt by the explosion. The shell cases were made of brass, and must have cost a great deal of money. Inside the outer brass case was a glass lining. Sometimes, even when a shell had been detonated, this glass lining would be found intact. The brass cases attracted us most, because people who were clever with their hands engraved or hammered on to them intricate patterns or floral designs. These horrible reminders decorated many mantelpieces in our village; serving as vases and spill jars. We spent hours searching the fields to find them and passed over all the beautiful flowers we only learned to value when we were older.

Because the work was so dangerous, a lot of money was paid to the women who spent their days or nights at the factory, though mother did not join their ranks — not for any moral reason, but because her sister who looked after our Grandma brought her to live with us. Grandma was over 80. She was a kind soul who always tried to be helpful, but was rather like a child who insists on 'doing it' before he is able. She had lost her memory, so forgot completely all the things she had been told. Our aunt came to help mother, who, having an 11-roomed house and three small children to cope with, as well as a smallholding, badly needed help. Grandma was really one person's work and if either auntie or mother was away from the house, looking after the children and Grandma was a full time job for the one who was left with them.

Father was paid 28/- a week, and on that we had to live and find food for the animals as well as for ourselves. Undaunted, mother and auntie set about rearing rabbits, chickens and ducks to sell for the table. Meat and grain were scarce and we grew giant sunflowers to help out the chickens' food supply, and extra potatoes. These also supplemented the meal given to the chickens. My sister and I were expected to gather a sack of dandelions and grass for the rabbits and goose-grass for the young geese. Goose-grass is horrible stuff. It has round, sticky little burrs all over it and stems covered in tiny hooks, which catch in hair and clothes. The goslings loved it chopped up with their grain or meal.

Just as the conversation among some young mothers these days will include the best food for babies, and the best method of rearing them, so during those war years it was likely to include the food for chickens, pigs and rabbits. There were many discussions on which were the best herbs to give rabbits. Dandelions, docks and sorrel were well known, but cow parsley was suspect. One of our neighbours killed all her rabbits by giving them hemlock instead of cow parsley. All sorts of misfortunes overtook us, but we plodded on.

In August and September there was a lot of fruit to be gathered, and mother and auntie would work away up in the trees, while my sister Naomi and I picked up the fallen fruit for use at home. They were frequently interrupted by Grandma, who would stagger up to the orchard, carrying the baby in her arms, having assured them, only half an hour previously, that she would not touch him. Grandma's efforts at helping once led to sheer panic. All by herself she had decided to take us for a walk while mother and auntie worked in the orchard. She donned her bonnet and shawl and my brother and sister were bundled into the pram, which, mercifully, did not tip over. I was to walk by the side of her.

The fruit pickers finished their work, and congratulating themselves on the state of calm down at the house, made their way there to get tea ready. They found an empty house; they called loudly but there was no answer. No sound met them. They looked at each other and then at the place where the pram was kept. It was empty! With hardly a word spoken they went out into the lane and each set off in a different direction. The village policeman was called in to help and pedalled off on his bicycle. Various neighbours joined the hunt. Eventually, the dear old lady was found about a mile away, happily pushing the pram. 'I was only going round the lanes', she said. Thank goodness she was discovered before coming to a very steep hill, where she could not possible have held the pram. She would probably have forgotten where she had come from and where she was going, even if her strength had lasted. Our village was full of problems in those days. When father returned, auntie took Grandma back to Bedford, and life for us at Lower Tuffley presented fewer hazards. Grandma lived for only a short while after returning home and auntie came back to us for a time before getting another job. She was a children's nurse and stayed with her families until the children were no longer in need of a nanny.

During the war years, mother and auntie worked early and late to earn the money to feed us all, but even so we had very little meat for our home use. We had an occasional rabbit or chicken, but these were generally taken, ready for the table, to a butcher's shop in the city. We had delicious casseroles, but there was very little butcher's meat. We consumed an enormous amount of boiled rice with jam and suet pudding. I hated both of them and only years later could I look at them without feeling sick.

An old friend killed the chickens, ducks and rabbits, and mother and auntie prepared them. The feathers flew in all directions when they had a large order to supply. Their fingers were red and sore from plucking the birds. When the rabbits were skinned and dressed and the chickens ready, they were loaded into the pram and mother, Naomi and I set off for Gloucester, two miles away. The butcher was always glad of our poultry and we got a good price for it. Naomi and I had to walk into Gloucester, though we sometimes got a lift in the pram on the return journey. Life was like this for everyone and there was no time to grumble. If our men were safe we were lucky. We children learned to pluck chickens and dress them and rabbits at an early age.

Having sold her rabbits and poultry, mother queued for cheese and butter. Because we were late, we were way back of the queue and often the butter and cheese had gone before we reached the counter. Rationing did not start at once in world War I, but things were much more fair when it was introduced.

Sometimes, when the grown-ups were very tired or depressed, we would hear them discussing whether one of them could go and work in the factory, but they never did.

However poor my mother was, she never forgot that we children did our best to help out, and when she had a little money, she would take us into Eastgate market, where we could choose one of the small toys for sale there. I had a succession of rag tabby cats which were filled with sawdust. This always dribbled out in the end, when the animal had been loved too much!

From time to time, when he was in France, Ernie would send us postcards of

French children surrounded by doves. I suppose they represented the dove of peace. The children were always beautifully dressed and we envied them their clothes. He also sent us silk envelopes embroidered in red, white and blue. They contained small greetings cards which we kept for years. Dad sent us cards occasionally with pictures of animals on the front. The message on the back was always the same — 'I hope you are well as this leaves me, love, Daddy'.

The aftermath of war made problems for everyone in Lower Tuffley. Men who had been in the forces for three or four years found it difficult to get back to the jobs they had left. These were not automatically held open for the returned soldiers at that time. Where jobs had been filled or were still being done by women it was not easy to find work, and unemployment took the place of the hazards that men had recently left. Women, having kept the home fires burning for three or four years, were loath to leave the interest of working outside the home; they were never to be as restricted again as they had been before 1914, so men had to compete. Even radiology, which had always been considered men's work at the Royal Infirmary, now had women in the X-Ray departments. They were as efficient as men at taking the photographs and developing results, sometimes using their own dark room at home.

We had one large room which had been designed to be a shop, but as our house was at the end of the village where the real country began, the shop was in the wrong place. So large a room had many uses, but during World War I the Mother's Union met there once a week for sewing classes. The ladies made and mended garments for soldiers. They probably enjoyed the opportunity of getting together to talk as such opportunities were infrequent in those days.

As our wounded soldiers came home, they overflowed our regular hospitals. At Tuffley, Dr Charles Lee Williams made a great contribution by providing a new small hospital. His wife was a Red Cross Commandant. It was promptly named the Red Cross Room and so we always knew it. I was taken once to see the hospital; it was a ward accommodating about ten soldiers, with a large kitchen and sterilizing unit. The small hospital was run most efficiently. The cleanliness was almost aggressive. Many people visited the soldiers and it was difficult to know which of us, the men or their visitors, were the more embarrassed. Somehow we felt terribly unable to say or do anything to compensate people, generally young, who had lost their limbs, or been gassed or badly wounded. We tried to thank and comfort them and did our best.

Sometime then I remember seeing an airship float over the village. It looked very beautiful, like a tremendous silver fish. It sailed so slowly and I remember thinking what an easy target it would make for people to shoot at. Young as I was, I thought it most unsafe.

Although I was only six when the Armistice was declared, I still have memories of that time which are very vivid. One concerned our first Christmas at home together as a family for three years. Most of the fathers who were lucky enough to be home and well, wanted their children to have the best Christmas they had ever known. We were told we were going to Gloucester and we could choose whichever thing we liked as our Christmas present. This was the most exciting idea to us and on the appointed day we trudged to the tram terminus and boarded a tram for Gloucester and started the fascinating search for the toy we liked the best. I settled for a teddy bear. He was only about fifteen inches long, but he was just what I wanted and his price was fifteen shillings, which was a lot of money in those days. He was my dearest possession for many years. He was nursed and taken to bed until I reached my teens and eventually he became bald and his stuffing came out. My sister had an Esquimo doll which was cheaper, so she chose a small pushchair to push it in. I forget what our brother had. The afternoon was very dark, even for December, and the pavements were wet and slushy from snow which was thawing. We thought it was the most wonderful afternoon we had ever known. The shops were all brightly lit and crammed with toys. Parents with children thronged the pavements, looking at the displays of toys with shining eyes. All parents demonstrated their happiness by giving their children a wonderful time.

The grocers' shops had an exciting smell in those days, combined of tea, coffee, spices, bacon, vegetables and soap. We miss so much in these days of prepackaging, when no aroma greets customers as they enter the great supermarkets. That first Christmas after the war the blended scents wafted out and on to the pavements, adding to people's delight. Toys were packed into huge shopping bags, to be put away until Christmas morning, and we made our way home out of the lighted streets and through the pitch dark of the country lanes.

Another memory of the early days after the war is of a beautiful sunny morning. It must have been the year after the Armistice was signed. We knew there was going to be a big parade of soldiers with bands and some kind of service to celebrate the ending of the war and my mother took my sister and me into Gloucester to see it. Although the autumn was passing, November was a beautiful month that year, sunny and warm during the day. All the able-bodied people in Lower Tuffley joined the trek into Gloucester and after the trams had put people down as near to the Cross as they could get, we all wanted to go closer. All the streets leading to the Cross, Eastgate, Southgate, Westgate and Northgate, were crowded for a distance of about a quarter of a mile. We all joined the people thronging the roads. Traffic had been stopped some way back. The centre of the streets was being cleared by mounted police so the pavements became densely packed.

The children, except those who were pushed to the front, saw little of what was going on, but we heard the band playing and the tramp, tramp, tramp of soldiers' feet. The band played the songs we had known all through the war — There's a long long trail a-winding into the land of my dreams, Keep the home fires burning, Lily of Laguna, The girl I left behind me — the band grew louder, passed us, and then gradually got fainter in the distance. Suddenly we heard the soldiers halt and stamp to attention. Orders were shouted all down the roads, far into the distance. We were quiet and listening for what would come next. The clock on the Cross struck eleven. Far away a bugle sounded the Last Post. Then there was complete silence. Among all those thousands of people, men, women, children, no one moved. The atmosphere was electric as from the oldest to the youngest of us, we remembered. After what seemed an age, Reveille was called, and all the people shifted a little. A great sigh went up from the crowd. 'O God our help in ages past', rose from the vast multitude. There were no amplifiers and the hymn started away in the distance and gradually reached us and we all joined in. Many people wept, some fainted — none forgot — ever.

Chapter Three Lanes, Fields and Footpaths

Our two lanes and the Stroud road formed a heart-shaped pattern, around which our lives revolved. The first quarter of this century still found us and our surroundings wild, compared with the tameness of the City. Not until the 'twenties was tarmac introduced as a road surface. During the war years, from 1914 to 1918, there was no advance in civilian living standards. All effort was directed towards winning the life-and-death struggle in which Britain, together with much of the rest of the world, was engaged. After the war, road repairs became an urgent necessity.

Until the introduction of the tar and stone road covering, one of our great interests was watching the huge steam-roller levelling granite stones to make a base for road repairs. All the steam-rollers were beautifully clean and their brasswork kept highly polished. They sucked up water from the brook to fill their boilers and a roaring fire was kept burning to raise the steam by which they were powered. They made a satisfying noise, clanking and grinding over the stones; their drivers and stokers enjoyed their jobs, but the men who shovelled the stones on to the surface of the road found it hard work. To the children watching, the procedure was enthralling. Small chippings and dust were watered in on top of the larger granite stones forming the base, and then the clanking steam-roller passed slowly over the new surface, levelling it in readiness for traffic. This made a very good road for horse-drawn vehicles, but when, later, the motor-car made its appearance, it soon proved unsuitable. For lesser repairs, heaps of granite stones were kept on the grass at the side of the road, and two roadmen worked continually, sitting on the heaps and knapping the large stones so that they were the right size to fill the puddles which formed in holes when it rained. The roadmen used long-handled hammers to break up the stones. They wore old coats and corduroy trousers, tied with string below their knees. They aged early and died young, the work being hard and monotonous and the men being exposed to all kinds of weather.

The lanes were winding and narrow; people with vehicles had to pull into gateways to let other loads pass. The verges were grass, into which iron-shod wheels sank deeply when the ground was wet. Most roads were bordered by ditches, which drained off surface water. They were sometimes quite deep, and to be 'ditched' was a common occurrence when two vehicles tried to pass each other. Thus life was always an adventure. People did not know what might befall them on a journey from the Stroud road to the Bristol road.

Increased motor traffic, however, brought inevitable changes. The old granite surface was too hard for rubber tyres and the top soon became bumpy and uneven. This led to the introduction of that mixture of tar and small stones, known as Tarmac, to give a gentler and smoother surface. Sometimes the tar was sprayed on to the road and the small stones shovelled on top. The tar gave off a wonderful smell for days afterwards. Main roads were repaired more frequently than the lanes and, being wider, did not provide so many hazards, but they, too, only had granite covering until the late 'twenties.

Colonel Edward Sinnott, who lived at Tuffley Grange, was the County Surveyor, responsible for all roads in the county. He joined the Forces as soon as war broke out and used his great organising ability in moving men and supplies in France until the War ended in 1918. When he returned, he found a tremendous task awaiting him in Gloucester. All the roads needed repairing at once. He set about rectifying this state of affairs as quickly as money and labour allowed and we village children had many hours of enjoyment watching the great rollers resurfacing the surrounding roads.

The lanes were a source of continual interest for us all. So many things happened in them. There was no fast traffic, but even so life was full of hazards. Bicycles were in everyday use then for many people and they gathered alarming speeds going down our steep hills. I was knocked down one day while meandering from one side of the road to the other. No harm was done except to clean clothes, and I was severely scolded for being so careless. These incidents gave life an excitement we miss now. There are bad accidents, but we have wide tarmac roads with pavements. Wild flowers and birds have been banished from them, leaving serviceable highways in place of our once lovely dangerous lanes.

Hedges along the old roadways were trimmed or laid infrequently, and, as they grew tall, they hoarded many delights. Violets grew under them in thick, scented clumps; so many that we could choose whether we would pick white ones or purple. I never found a violet perfume which matched their sweet fragrance.

Spring did not come to Lower Tuffley at any special date, but when the banks of a ditch which ran along the side of Tuffley Lane, from the Court to the row of houses below it, shone with celandines, their enamelled golden petals reflecting the lustre of spring sunshine. No matter how often that ditch was cleaned, the celandines always survived, to reappear next Spring. The heavy early rains made the ditches muddy and full, but the water was always crystal clear the next day.

Cow parsley flowered in great patches; we called its flowers 'Ladies' Needlework', and gathered great bunches to go with the golden buttercups which grew all along the lanes. We never tired of putting a flower under a friend's chin to see the golden reflection. We said that person 'liked butter'. An overhang of wild roses in one of the tall hedges filled the lane with beautiful pink colour and a haunting fragrance, while further along bushes of white tea roses gave off a completely different but equally lovely scent. Meadowsweet and elder flowers filled the air with golden pollen and a cloying perfume. May blossom covered the hedges like snow, while two beautiful May trees were rose red, and the flowers double instead of single. There were occasional horse chestnut trees, both pink and white. These gave us conkers in the Autumn. Children still tie them on strings and try and hit each other's conker until one of them breaks.

Autumn brought berries, deep red on the hawthorn bushes; scarlet hips where the dog roses had bloomed. Birds built their nests in every hedge and often the bushes were too thick for them to be seen. The girls tried to ignore them, so that the boys would not find them, but we were not often successful.

The banks of the railway line running from Gloucester, along the back of the village on its way to London, were always an attraction to us. Perhaps because we knew that climbing the embankment was dangerous and forbidden, it became all the more desirable. There were arches over Tuffley Lane and Grange Road; the Grange Road one was curved, so we could not see the opposite end. Continual hazards were provided here by stray horses, cows and carts; while a loaded hay waggon filled the aperture, so none could pass.

Tiny ferns grew in the crevices between the stones with which the arch was faced. We tried, in vain, to get them to grow at home. They liked the mortar and could not survive in ordinary soil. On the embankment grew flowers that we found nowhere else in Lower Tuffley, such as toadflax, with its delicate stems and its orange and lemon flowers. Early in Spring, coltsfoot and bladder campion flourished there.

Sometimes we put crossed pins and coins on the metals and waited until a train passed over them. The pins were flattened into the shape of a pair of scissors and the coins (halfpennies generally) were several sizes larger after treatment! We never had an accident doing this but later on children who climbed the embankment were killed under the trains. We must have led charmed lives.

Two very different kinds of animal and insect life inhabited this bridge. In the luminous dusk of summer evenings, just as darkness approached, hundreds of bats, as if at a given signal, would fly out from their hiding places under the arch. Their shrill screams were audible to children, but to many older people, whose hearing was not so acute, their cries were too high pitched to be heard. We watched fascinated as they shot out and then darted about in all directions, never colliding, catching the flies which danced in the warm air.

The other attraction of this place at night was glow-worms. All along a low bank lining one side of the bridge, as dark came down on spring evenings, small, fiery, greenish points of light would appear. We never, at that time, found what caused them; the small beetles responsible disappeared when people tried to find them. I saw one only once, and it was quite tiny, yet able to give so much light.

The embankment was responsible for a great deal of trespassing and illicit finds on the part of local children, though one day when a group of us had been foraging, no one seemed to find anything unusual. But later on, when my sister went to bed, a terrified scream came from her room and we rushed in to see what had happened. A slow worm had been carefully hidden between the sheets! My brother had retired early that night, and he was suspiciously deaf and later on his bedroom door was found to be locked. The creature was put outside in the grass, where it wriggled away, so it could not have suffered from its adventure!

The bridge was built on land which was always wet and boggy. Rushes and wild peppermint grew there in abundance. These were gathered by gypsies. The rushes they plaited to use in making various articles including mats and baskets. The peppermint was sold in small bottles as essence. They called at our houses two or three times each year with baskets of pegs, (made by the men), lace, tape, elastic, needles and pins plus their herb remedies. These were most welcome in days when no National Health Service existed, and doctors' fees were beyond the means of some of us.

In addition to the gypsies a regular caller was the umbrella lady. Her name was Mrs Loveridge. She was a much loved grandmother of a family who lived on a piece of land forming the corner of the Bristol road with Tuffley Lane. The brook formed its boundary. Mrs Loveridge visited us two or three times each year with umbrellas. Sometimes she had refurbished our own worn ones, some would be those she had taken in part-exchange, and mended to sell again, while some were our worn-out brollies which she would use as spare parts. Her money was kept in a pocket under the white apron which always covered her black clothes. She and her family lived in some railway carriages and an old-fashioned caravan. The carriages and the van were always spotlessley clean, with lace curtains at all the windows and shining brass and paintwork on the van. Mrs Loveridge owned all of them. She lived to be a great age and worked for most of her life. The little settlement brought colour and interest to what had been a rather dull corner.

The fields were our roaming territory. We found interest all the year round in them. Sometimes flowers, or other people's apples, blackberries, mushrooms, and occasionally a real adventure like the sheep which had rolled over onto its back and was helplessly stuck. It had a worn patch of grass completely bare in its great efforts to right itself. We helped it to turn over and get up and watched while it slowly hobbled away to join the flock. We told the farmer in case it needed his attention but instead of thanking us for saving its life, he demanded angrily, 'What were you doing trespassing over there?'

We knew the names of most of the fields, of which some were very old—Roundham, Longround, Fourteen Acres, the Beany, the Marsh—the list is endless. We found cowslips and bluebells in Spring, giving way to moon daisies and totty grass in Summer. At school there were wide windowsills, always filled with jars of flowers from the fields. The were two bushes of spurge laurel growing in one hedge, but some instinct told us not to touch the beautiful waxen flowers—only to look. The bush, although we were not aware of it, is deadly poison. In one field, patches of rest harrow (so named because of its wiry, thorny stems) made splashes of rose pink from one end to the other when the pea-shaped flowers were in bloom. We were unable to pick these. The Beany was a field where beans for cattle food were once grown. The perfume from the flowers of the beans spread all over the neighbouring meadows in the evenings. The Marsh, as its name suggests, was always wet and boggy.

Larks used to rise, singing, from almost under our feet, but their nests were so well hidden that we never found one. Partridges make their nests on the ground, too, in rough grass and one could almost tread on them before seeing them. The young ones are so well camouflaged that they are nearly undetectable against their background.

A root of meadow cranesbill survived for many years against a bridge which spanned Sandford's brook. This brook formed the boundary between Lower Tuffley and Quedgeley. It was dammed to supply water to Tuffley Farm, and thus provided the village children with an open-air swimming pool. We spent many long, lazy afternoons swimming and lying in the grass on sunny Summer days. We just hoped that no one drank the water afterwards, but as the stream ran through the dam, the water was constantly being changed. The ram pump, which pumped the water up to the farm, rarely worked in the afternoons. Other farmers, living below the dam, got very angry over it; they said the dam deprived them of their rightful share of the water. We never knew that brook to run dry, and fish of different kinds lived in it, so probably the farmers were just jealous that one of their number had had the good sense to make the most use of the water. It was piped to tanks in various fields, so that the cattle and horses always had enough water and no longer had to depend on ponds.

Mushrooms and blackberries in season we picked every year. As my friend Lilian says, 'Oh happy days!'.

Carew Tyler, eldest daughter of Colonel Sinnott, reminded me about the ponds. She says 'I remember the lovely variety of little ponds there were. There were newts in the deep one bordering our drive. We spent hours at the dew-pond down in the orchard under that lovely oak, a safe distance from the house. We kept our punt there.'

I remember that punt very well. We paddled it round the edge of the pond until it filled with water and began to sink (anno domini had made it very leaky), then it had to be baled out before proceeding.

Most of the fields had their own ponds and each one was different. Each one teemed with life, animal and vegetable. Some of the deeper ones had moorhens and there were two secret ones, surrounded by dense hedges. One of these was on Whaddon Green, opposite a farm where a family called Smart lived. There was a story attached to it. We told it in shocked undertones while leaning on the locked gate, over which we got the only glimpse to be seen of the pond. It was circular, with steep sides, about six foot high. In Spring they were covered with primroses. The story ran that once, a long time ago, a little boy had been drowned in that pond and they found him floating, face upwards. That was why the hedge had been planted and why the flowers had been set in the banks. We looked and imagined we could see the white face of the little boy as he floated in the deep, dark water. It was certainly one of the dangerous ponds. It had a counterpart down in the fields; hedged and secret, the home of moorhens. This belonged to the same estate, so possibly the owner had thought these ponds too dangerous to leave open. Animals would easily have drowned in them. The one in the fields was also used as a well; there was a pumphouse quite near, which would be another reason for its being secluded.

One pool lay along the lane and it was full of pond weed of the kind which is sold for aquariums. Its depths were too dark and screened for us to see the bottom, but dragonflies hovered and darted above it, their shining wings and bodies scintillating in the sunlight, giving off shafts of indigo blue light. We often arrived late at school because we had been watching this pool.

Some of the deep ponds were breeding grounds for newts and the boys fished for them with worms tied on string, with rods made of sticks. The newts were easily caught, poor things, though most of them were put back into the water. Some of them which my brother caught were put in a fish-pond that I had made, with disastrous results. They bit off the fish's tails and fins. The pond had to be emptied and the newts returned to their own habitat. My brother loved introducing fresh life into my pond, and when he caught several carp he carried them home in water and slid them in with the goldfish. They interbred and the result was huge black fish which turned golden after a year or two.

The flowers surrounding and in the ponds varied a good deal, and we found a lot of interest in going from one to another comparing the different species. Pond crowfoot covered one which was edged with water plantains.

There was one pool which had a really tragic history. Robinswood Hill had a quarry where clay was dug to make the bricks of which so many of the houses in the valley for miles round, as well as along the base of the hill, had been built. A deep hole at the bottom of the pit was always filled with water. We were continually warned to keep away from the clay-face, but climbing around the edges of the quarry was a challenge, to the boys particularly. Several fell in the water at different times. Mr Pritchard, the subpostmaster, was adept at resuscitation and rescued several boys who otherwise would have died. Then one day, word was brought to him that one of his twin sons had fallen in and, although he had been pulled out, was unconscious. Mr Pritchard ran, as he always did, in spite of the fact that he was a heavy man. He worked with the intensity of desperation on his boy — without avail. Cyril never recovered consciousness. We all sensed the cruel irony of Mr and Mrs Pritchard's loss. He had given so many people back their sons, but could not save his own.

Rumours spread rapidly and at school assembly that morning Mr Herrin confirmed the tragedy, told us the whole story and asked us not to speak of it to Cyril's brother, Percy, when he returned to school unless he himself wanted to talk about it. We gave our word, and as far as I know, none did intrude into the family's grief.

Ours was a small school of about 150 pupils, so we were rather like a large family and when one part of us was in distress, we all shared in it.

There is no doubt that the ponds were dangerous, but gave us so much interest and fun. On the larger ones we slid as ice formed thickly in winter. A dozen or more of us would 'keep the pot boiling', never letting the slide be empty of a slider. This, too, was dangerous, when the ice was thawing or too thin in the centre.

The Ministry of Agriculture hated ponds. They said they were insanitary and should all be filled in. This could not be done while there was no alternative water supply, but once we did have piped water, the powers-that-be filled in all our lovely ponds and their loss took some of the old character from our village.

There were many footpaths through Lower Tuffley connecting the village with Gloucester and all the surrounding districts. We used them whenever the weather allowed, because until I was in my teens, there was no bus and even cycles were a very precious commodity. Because we walked a great deal, we had time to be much more observant than our modern counterparts, who are taken everywhere so often by car. They miss all the small happenings in the countryside, through no fault of their own; but progress, which rules out the opportunity to stop and look when some such small happening takes place, or to watch a rare wild flower opening its petals, does not give time for looking.

We never returned from any walk without bringing something home — it might be catkins or grasses, it might not be anything tangible, but just knowledge — and I still have the habit of looking closely at everything I pass while out walking.

While many of our footpaths were quite straight, others meandered hither and thither, and we divided them roughly into two separate categories — those which got us somewhere quicker than the lanes, and those which simply offered pleasure. Several of our paths headed straight for Gloucester and were worn deeply, because people needed them for their everyday work and for going shopping. One went from our orchard to the Stroud road; going the other way it led to Quedgeley. We used a footpath to cut half a mile off the journey to Whaddon Church, this path was full of interest as well.

The straight pathway from the back of our orchard to the Stroud road cut a longer distance off, and in the summer we sometimes found a bee orchid in one of the hedges which bordered it. This came up in the middle of the hedge year after year.

Most of these paths had been ancient tracks, and were, at least, hundreds of years old. Roads have replaced them now. The lanes are tamed and the teeming life of the ponds stifled under the tons of earth shovelled in by the mechanical digger. The people who live in the houses which cover the lost countryside will never see the beauty which once was there.

Chapter Four Orchards and a Brook

The orchards of Lower Tuffley were the frills on the skirts of our village; frothy scallops of pink and white during April and May, canopies of green leaves hung with ripening plums, apples and pears in September; food for body and soul.

The Victoria and Pershore plums kept pickers busy in the early days of the month; in the glut years we sold many before they were ripe, to ease the boughs weighed down to breaking point with fruit, and to help the growth of those which were left. Green plums cook well, but are rather bitter and require a lot of sugar to sweeten them. Only the best fruit would sell in a year of great plenty. At such times, many villagers turned their fruit into home-made wine and cider. We all made wine of different kinds and there was great rivalry as everyone tried to outdo his neighbour. Some liked it sweet, some preferred it dry, everyone wanted his own particular favourite to be as strong as possible.

As our plums ripened, wine making and jamming and bottling gathered momentum. We all laid by a store for the winter, and if there was any over, it could go to bazaars, or be kept for the next year, which would probably be much leaner. The number of wasps increased as the month progressed and exterminating the nests occupied the time of the big boys. They would smoke the nests to stupify the wasps, and then dig out the cake holding the grubs ready to hatch out. These were used as bait for fishing.

Ours was a great village for producing perry and cider. Most of the pear trees bore fruit for perry, while every orchard had its cider apples. The pears never became soft, even when ripe; they remained as hard as bullets until the inside turned brown and 'sleepy'. The children at the Grange, in the farms and the village all indulged in pear fights. These could be dangerous to life and limb and, in the days before detergents were invented, had catastrophic effects on our clothes. They left deep brown stains, which refused to disappear however many times they were washed. The perry trees grew to a great height and, while some people struggled to erect forty-foot ladders against them, most preferred to wait until the fruit fell down, which could be quite late in the autumn. It was then gathered into sacks and stacked under the trees to await transportation.

We took our perry pears in turn to Mr Savage at Tuffley Farm, who owned an enormous stone cider press and coped with most local people's fruit. The press filled one end of a covered barn. Pears or apples were poured into the trough and then the screw of the great stone press was made to revolve (I believe it was pushed round manually) until the fruit was ground up and became a dry and solid mass. The juice ran down into a huge tub and was then poured into the owner's casks. Carew Tyler tells how the children at the Grange sucked the juice through straws inserted in a bung-hole, until they became slightly tipsy, in spite of threats of castor oil.

Hot cider was supposed to be a cure for measles and I well remember sitting up in bed, all red and rashy, with my sister (who was expected to catch measles and didn't) and brother, all drinking hot cider. I hated it, but it made us perspire a great deal and probably helped to 'bring the rash out'.

No sugar was added to either perry or cider and often draught ciders are very tart. They are extremely potent and people who have stomach ailments are well advised never to drink them. There is an old saying that when people get drunk on Gloucester cider, they take one step forward and two steps back!

Some of the deep red and light green cider apples were delicious. The little Bitter Sweets were really sweet and always crisp. Every year children got into trouble through stealing them. We raided one orchard most afternoons when we were let out of school, until one fateful day. The trees in Mr Smart's orchard were old and bent; they were that much easier to climb. On this day, my sister had been hoisted up into a tree and was busily shaking down apples for us, while we collected them below. We had curious storage places for them. The girls often filled the legs of their navy bloomers (the elastic had to be good), while the boys filled first their pockets and then the tops of their socks. On this day, we were all absorbed in picking up the apples and hiding them on our persons, so that no one heard the footsteps of a horse quietly picking its way along the other side of the hedge, until, with a shout from his rider and a whinny from the animal, they came crashing through the half-open gate into the orchard. The farmer realised as he caught sight of us—caught in the act—that what he had suspected for a long time was only too true!

We all fled, spilling our ill-gotten gains as we ran—all except my poor sister, who was marooned in the tree. She, sitting and quaking, got the rough end of the farmer's tongue, although he told her that, as the rest of us had got away, he would content himself with telling our schoolmaster about our misdeeds in the morning.

We watched for him anxiously the next day and, sure enough, about eleven o'clock in the morning we saw the farmer approaching the school. He and our head were closeted together for a long time before he eventually left. We were given time to wonder and worry and our anxiety increased by the minute until, at the beginning of the afternoon, when all the children were assembled in the hall prior to dispersing to our separate classrooms, Mr Herrin's lecture came.

'Boss' Herrin, as he was known, did not get his name for nothing. He could be scathing and reduce us to abject misery when he liked, and this time he liked very much! He kindly said that he would name no names, although he knew which of us were concerned; but if ever he had another complaint, whether we were boys or girls, we would be sorry we had ever been born. He mentioned no particular punishment, but he was very good at inventing those and we were in no doubt that he would keep his word to the letter. Much as we loved those apples, we left them alone ever afterwards.

One orchard which was very tempting belonged to Mr Charlie Jones of Glencoe, a large double-fronted house in Grange Road. His trees bordered the lane and the apples on them were the biggest and juiciest in the whole village. They were beautiful; red and yellow and full of flavour. Charlie never picked them, but allowed them to fall and rot in the longish grass beneath his trees. There they lay, a tremendous temptation to every child who passed. If we did not see him and thought the coast was clear, we dived over the stile in the hedge enclosing his orchard, through which a footpath ran, and made for the nearest fallen apple.

Although we could not see him, we never knew for certain where Mr Jones would be lurking, and more than once he crashed out from under the trees, shotgun at the ready. We never found out if it was loaded or not, but as he was a very bulky person and could not run very much, he pretended he would shoot us. If he had put a basket of apples at his gateway for children to take, no one would have tried to steal, but it was infuriating to have to watch those apples lying in the grass day by day until they rotted away.

Charlie just couldn't understand why we should want to rob his orchard when so many of us had apple trees of our own. Our own fruit was never so enticing as Charlie Jones's was. He finally settled the matter by winding barbed wire all over his stile, and for many months no one was able to use the footpath.

The orchard trees were the roofs below which thrived many kinds of life. The land on which the trees stood was used to rear all sorts of poultry and animals. Pigs often ran loose and rooted up the grass in the summer, making a quagmire of the ground in wet weather, when they were aided and abetted by the ducks. At the Grange, Colonel Sinnott had perry trees to produce wine for the house and his orchards supported poultry and sometimes sheep. Occasionally, when our grazing became poor, or we wanted to keep grass for hay, we rented one of his orchards for extra feed for the horses.

The Colonel's mind was always bent on organising for the finest results and gradually, between the wars, he planted a new orchard with the finest apple trees he could buy. He did not stop at the orchard. Much to his gardener's disgust, he occasionally bought a fine specimen to be planted in the garden. Mr Merriman, realising that more trees meant fewer vegetables, then withdrew into himself and indulged in a lengthy sulk, until something else took his attention.

The Colonel next worked out that all those trees would require colonies of bees to pollinate the apple blossom and accordingly invested in several hives. His bees were certainly fine examples of industry. They swarmed frequently, often on summer Sunday afternoons, when the village had relapsed into sabbatical calm and repose. As we dozed in our deck chairs or on our beds, we would suddenly be galvanised into action by the buzzing of many thousands of bees' wings which, combined, made a noise like a rushing stream. This sound would be accompanied by a loud banging of some instrument on a tin tray or a gong.

A swarm of bees leaves the hive either because it has become over populated or because there are too many queens in it. One queen is enough, but among the eggs she lays there may be other queens. The old queen and her faithful followers leave the hive to find another home. For several days previous to this, the hive will have been restless, and many workers and drones will have been waiting outside it for the queen to emerge. She finally comes out, followed by thousands of bees; usually they do not go very far, but if the swarm flies high, the distance can be as much as two miles. They then settle, while some of the drones fly off to find a suitable home.

There is an old English law which lays it down that as long as the owner of the bees follows them, banging on a tray, no one else can claim them. The banging is also supposed to persuade the bees to land, but the bees themselves have never confirmed this!

A swarm would sometimes settle in one of our trees, and then we would watch them carefully. Usually they quickly cluster round the queen in a deep heaving, living mass, each one clings to the bees under it. It was amazing that no bees ever got hurt or suffocated. They would gradually quieten until, in the evening, Colonel Sinnott would arrive, covered from head to foot and carrying a smoke gun in case the bees were restive. He held a skep under the mass, and smartly shook the bough, when they all dropped off into the container. They were quickly covered and taken back to a hive already prepared for them, to start their cycle of breeding and producing honey all over again. We enjoyed the combs of honey which came our way from time to time and the bees provided a great interest—if only they had not chosen Sunday afternoon to swarm.

When the Colonel's apple trees matured, they produced enormous crops which went a long way towards supplying the needs of a local wholesale greengrocer. The apples and the bees relied on each other for support and the resulting harvests filled the requirements of many people living in Gloucester.

The Grange orchard had one other tree which no one else in the village possessed—a tall walnut tree. Every autumn the nuts fell down in a brown circle around it, then the girls came from the house and picked the nuts up with their bare feet. We ordinary children envied them much more for being allowed to run about all day with bare feet than we did for having a walnut tree. Our parents were very conservative about bare feet; they believed we would get cuts and bruises. The people at the Grange were more enlightened. Gradually we too were allowed to go without shoes while on grass.

In our own orchard, as well as fruit trees we kept poultry of all sorts and pigs. Once we had a lamb—an orphan that dad brought home in his pocket from the farm. Billy, as he was called, had a bottle and was fed on milk; his tail quivered with delight as he sucked it up. He had to have a wooden teat in the bottle because, as his teeth grew, he chewed the rubber ones to pieces. He developed quickly and soon became the local bully. His butting and general bad habits eventually forced my father to send him to market. I was very sad to watch Billy following the shepherd who drove the other sheep in front of him. Billy trusted us because we had reared him. In those days, most animals walked to the market in droves, holding up all the traffic as they went. It caused a nightmare situation. Not until motor traffic and huge cattle trucks took over was this rectified.

Dogs are notorious for chasing sheep; my sister had a golden cocker pup called Puck which chased everything that moved. He was usually kept out of the orchard, but one day he managed to squeeze in behind Naomi and his mischievous mind at once grasped the situation. He singled out one chicken and stalked it. Of course, the bird ran fluttering its wings and squawking loudly. The pup chased after it. In vain my sister called him back; the more the hen ran, the faster he chased it, absolutely deaf to his mistress's shouts of distress. Eventually he caught up with the bird, which stopped suddenly. Puck rolled over it, and the bird lay limp on the ground. The dog lost interest. My sister caught him and he had a sound spanking; then she ran down to the house to tell mother. Mother was always practical. 'Hide the poor thing', she said, 'and take it home with you when you go. It will make you a dinner tomorrow'. We were terrified that my father would find the bird. She hid it and later father left for the farm to fetch the afternoon's milk. Naomi went to retrieve the bird, but could not find anything in the corner where she had hidden it. She looked around and eventually saw it, peacefully feeding with the other hens. Her anxiety turned to fury. 'That fool of a pup', she said, 'after worrying me stiff, couldn't even do the job properly'. The hen had only been stunned. It saved explanations later. Our lives were never dull.

Through many of the orchards ran the brook, on its way to meet the Gloucester to Sharpness Canal. We never knew its name, but referred to it as 'the Brook' or the 'River Tuff'. Older people called it other names, depending on what mischief we had been up to in the stream. Often to them it was 'That Dirty Ditch'. To us children, it was our dearest playmate.

The brook crossed under the Stroud road near the school and bordered Grange Road for about a quarter of a mile, when it turned at a right angle and, for the next mile or so, ran through meadows and orchards, under the railway line, under our lane, to meander through the fields and orchards between us and the canal.

It had cut a very deep channel for itself; it was a swift stream, usually about two feet wide and three inches deep, normally very clear and clean. After heavy rain or melting snow, however, this friendly watercourse could become a muddy, raging torrent, up to six feet deep in places and extremely dangerous.

Where it ran beside the road, it was marked by poles and piping. These constituted our gymnasium; we turned over the pipes with endless variations, boys and girls alike. The boys teased the girls unmercifully about their underclothes — usually bloomers. In those days only the boys wore trousers and even then they were shorts until the boys reached eleven or twelve. Of course, the boys always wanted to wear long trousers earlier than they were allowed to, and parents then were faced with the argument that 'everybody' except the hard-done-by boy in question wore long pants. The age gradually came down until short trousers at ordinary schools were rare.

We girls did not worry much about the boys' teasing. We executed complicated twists and turns on the poles, enjoying ourselves and completely forgetting how time was passing.

Bamping was another game with the brook. It consisted of jumping from one side to the other, widening the jump each time until inevitably someone fell in and got wet feet. The boys used long poles which gave them a wonderful flying leap. Bamping when the brook was in flood was extremely dangerous, and only the boys attempted it, while the girls cheered them on. Flood water always produced 'Monkey soap' — a collection of foam caused by all sorts of flotsam brought down by the raging current.

We used to cause a good deal of trouble by collecting this junk and, adding it to a small blockage, made a dam which could flood the lane. Then everyone got wet feet and our parents were furious.

We played Pooh Sticks, and sailed paper boats on the brook, and we were often late home from school. Anxious parents, who came looking for the children who should have been home long ago, usually found them absorbed in some game in which the brook figured.

The most dangerous game we played was crawling through a culvert, which was built across a corner formed by the Tuff to carry away the flood water. We took advantage of low water to do this. The culvert was semi-circular, so that when one reached the middle, it was quite dark. There was only just room to crawl and the game was satisfyingly hair raising.

One wet winter day, when most children (including our family) had stayed at school for lunch, the brook nearly claimed one of our horses as its victim. The few children who had been home came back late and all excited about what they had been watching.

Our mare, Bess, was sharing Colonel Sinnott's old orchard at the time, grass being in short supply in ours. She must have gone to the brook for water as usual and, not realising how deep the water was, had slipped down the steep bank and was standing up to her neck in it. She had tried repeatedly to climb out, slipping back on the wet clay each time, until she could no longer get any purchase, and her strength against the strong current was ebbing.

Fortunately a passer-by caught sight of her, or she must have been drowned. As it was, my father and several helpers had put a rope round her and had tried to pull her out, without any success. One man stood in that fast-flowing, dangerous stream, up to his shoulders in icy, muddy water, holding Bess's head clear for over an hour. They next harnessed Tommy and tied a rope between the two horses, but could still make no headway. Then, as was the way of our village, without being asked and having got word of what was going on, Mr King from Tuffley Farm sent a tractor with its driver, and between them they managed to pull the horse clear.

The next difficulty was in getting her to stand. The vet was called and, after drying Bess as far as they could, she had to be walked around for some time, after which a sling was hung from the roof of the barn. She remained in the sling for three days before she was able to walk properly. She finally recovered, but had lost so much strength that she was never able to pull a load again and we had to sell her to someone who needed a horse for light work only.

Many years later, when houses were encroaching on our meadows, the brook was piped into a culvert. When the locals saw the size of the pipes, they told the authorities that they were not nearly large enough to take flood water. They were laughed at, but were later proved correct. When a specially bad storm arises, or prolonged rain or snow raises the level of the brook, it floods the lower houses in the estate which has grown up over Colonel Sinnott's old orchard.

Like most of our playmates the brook has gone — perhaps for ever.

Chapter Five Horses In Our Village

During the early part of the century, horses shared the work of the farm with men every day. They pulled carts filled with roots, hay waggons, harvesting machines and vehicles of many types in which people travelled from place to place. They are beautiful animals to watch and there is no lovelier sight than two or three great horses drawing a plough, guided by their ploughman, turning shining furrows of wet earth.

The team would be followed by hundreds of seagulls, just as the tractor is today. They wheeled in a screaming, seething white cloud just above the newly turned earth, watching for worms and grubs; their whiteness accentuated by a grey, lowering sky. There would be a target to reach before dusk descended; horses and man knew their job and they worked at a deceptively steady pace to achieve their goal. But the toil was hard for man and horses alike and, although some of the beautiful Shires and Percherons are still sometimes to be seen ploughing, farmers, on the whole, have welcomed the tractor.

The days when a ploughman and his horses worked as a team were very satisfying and their steady pace continued until the light faded. The tractor has not the heart of a horse and man team, it is man's tool, not his friend. There is much less beauty and less satisfaction to be had from driving a combine harvester than a horse-drawn machine, steadily leaving its straight lays of grass or grain.

The Gloucestershire farms had their share of fine working horses, and there are still many of them pulling farm implements today.

The horses at the farm nearest our village — Tuffley Farm — were well kept and an impressive bunch. They worked all day during the week and were turned out in the fields at night. There, for a time, they would graze and drink and rest; but, for some reason, occasionally a spirit of mischief would spread among them. Sometimes one of them would lift the five-barred gate off its latch or, if it was padlocked, they would worry at a thin place in the hedge until they made a 'shard', as our village people called it. 'Shard', an old English word for 'gap', was still in use, together with many just as old, when I was young. When the gap was large enough, the horses filed out in an orderly manner — and then all restraint ended. With heads thrown up, they whinnied and snorted and stampeded towards the village. It was always a frightening experience to watch them approaching, galloping all over the road and verges, manes and tails streaming; if they came from the far side of the railway bridge, they thundered through it and the sound was deafening. The bridge gave off a satisfying echo (it was well tested by the local children), but the noise those horses produced was nothing less than terrifying. Often they did this at night and the whole village would suddenly be startled out of sleep by the sound of their coming. The horses enjoyed the din they made and until they found an open gate they continued their clattering way through the village.

Woe betide anyone whose gate was not closed. However fast they ran, the leader would see it and turn in at the gateway followed by the rest of them. The luckless owner's garden would be reduced to rubble and a few remaining plants, very quickly. On one occasion Colonel Sinnott's gate had not been shut and up the drive they pounded, across his lawn and tennis court, making a wide trail of hoof marks, which doubled as they returned, leaving destruction in their wake. The damage was not fully repaired for many months.

Coming into the lane again, they continued through the village until either they reached the end of the houses, or someone turned them back. Once turned, their wild spirits seemed to evaporate and they would walk or trot back comparatively quietly, reaching their heads over hedges and fences to take any greenery to which they were attracted. Reaching their farmyard in the early hours of the morning, the horses waited patiently until someone heard them and let them into the orchard, where they stayed until it was time to begin the day's work. The damage they had done, and the noise they made was always a good topic of conversation over the garden hedges the next day.

By day, when they were separated, these beautiful, mischievous animals were very docile and good-natured, and my sister, who had always been afraid of large animals, would ride one great grey horse and lead another from farm to farm as they were needed first in one place and then another.

We never had a large horse of our own. For our work, which was mainly concerned with the milk-round, the smaller horses were better. When mowing or some heavy job required larger ones, we borrowed one, together with the necessary machine, and usually their farmer sent his man with them. There were several horses at different times; they came, stayed awhile, and were sold again. They were measured against our 'steady' Tommy.

Tommy was a little rough-coated sturdy Welsh cob. He was with us from the time he was three years old until he died at something over twenty-five. Like all the other favourite friends, human or animal, he was always given the prefix 'Old'. It is a widespread custom when people are fond of someone to refer to him or her as 'Old' so-and-so.

Old Tom was full of character. He was willing, but liked his own way if he could get it; he was very good-natured, especially with children, and he never bore a grudge. But he was no fool. The grown-ups often told the tale of Old Tom standing stock-still, while one of their children, aged about fourteen months, hung round his legs and kissed him. None dared call either to the child or the horse in case Tom moved his foot. He knew this was not the moment to move and remained like a statue until the loving finished and the baby wandered away.

He had one fault which caused us a great deal of trouble. He disliked any new horse we had. This was shortsighted on his part, because other horses were there to share the work and give him more rest. He was probably jealous. This was his home and any other horse was an interloper. His bad behaviour, biting and kicking, led to his having to be kept away from other horses, which made life complicated, as we had so little space. My father put a fence across the middle of the paddock and tried to keep one horse one side and one the other, but they still quarrelled and from time to time Old Tom had to be kept in the orchard. He didn't mind, he knew exactly when the apples were fit to eat and on which tree. He always looked carefully to see if anyone was watching him and, if he thought the coast was clear, up would go his head into the tree, biting off apples and crunching them up until his mouth was thickly rimmed in foam. He shook a lot down and, if pigs were loose in the orchard, he would be surrounded by them as they cashed in on his ingenuity and cleared up all the fallings. Of course we watched and when we caught him we would shout, 'Tommy!' Immediately his head came down and he was innocently grazing. When he came to the tree, he would rub himself vigorously against the trunk, which shook the fruit down in showers and he had apples galore. He could never hide his gluttony, his mouth always gave him away.

He had great intelligence and when our father fell asleep in the milk float after a long hard morning, Old Tom would keep going and bring the float and its contents — with driver — safely home, often through traffic, to a standstill in the yard.

Once he misjudged the width of the cart and hit our oak gate-post with the wheel hub. Father woke up frightened, and poor Tom got the rough end of his temper. Once when dad had stayed talking longer than Tom considered necessary, he thought his driver was asleep as usual and brought the float and its load of cans, eggs and bottles safely home. We were alarmed to see no father in the float and realised that if he had been left behind, he would be furious; so we hurried to unharness Tom and turn him out in the paddock. Somehow we placated our father on his return. He was tired — too tired to go out after the horse who had made a mistake.

As soon as we children were big enough, around ten years old, we were expected to take the horses into Gloucester to the blacksmith to be shod when they needed it. Often the blacksmith would have an hour free in the afternoons. With the other horses this was just a routine job, but Old Tom was different. He was an individual; he knew we were young and inexperienced and he insisted in going round at least some of the roads he usually traversed in the mornings. To us this constituted a nightmare. Whoever was unfortunate enough to be chosen as driver tugged at the reigns and shouted at him. In vain. Tom got the bit between his teeth and trotted steadily on in the direction he wished to go until he was tired of it and eventually agreed to go the way his driver wanted him to. We usually got him to the blacksmith just on time.

The smithy was dark after the sun outside and warm from the forge. The blacksmith wore a thick leather apron. Except for the re-heating and finishing, a set of shoes was always ready for Old Tom, who lifted each foot in turn, standing quite quietly while they were trimmed and fitted. His hooves were blacked and polished and he always looked comfortable and smart when shoeing was finished. The smithy also coped with making the iron tyres which were used on most of our vehicles then, and we watched, fascinated, as the almost red-hot tyres were shrunk on to the wooden wheels by immersing them, wheels and all, in cold water. There was a tremendous hissing, and clouds of steam arose, which shut out sight of the smithy for a minute or two. The resulting fit was always good. The smell of that smithy was unforgettable, a mixture of leather, coke, burning horn and sizzling iron.

After he had been shod and reharnessed, Tom was turned head-for-home. Going home was easy. The baker's horse and the milkman's horse are much the same, they both know their way home. We reached home with all possible speed and, once loose, Tom would kick up his heels in the air and gallop round the field, enjoying the comfort of his newly shod feet.

Old Tom had two pet hates: newspaper or white paper blowing about round his feet, and the sound of the Salvation Army band. These two things scared him beyond reasoning. He would throw up his head and, giving a loud frightened whinny, launch himself forward, trying to move beyond the terror which gripped him. He shied and cavorted, and there was no hope of restraining him until judged he was safe. The float, with all its contents, hurtled along behind him, with father vainly trying to stop the horse, while he held on to milk urns, set overturned cans upright, salvaged bottles etc., and tried not to see dozens of broken eggs. Tom wouldn't stop until his terror had abated, and by the time it did, a quantity of damage had usually been done. Father was reduced to fury and we shrank away in terror and to try and calm him down ran at the double with our milk deliveries. The Salvation Army band Tommy would hear when it was streets away and we learned to dread helping dad on Sunday mornings. The poor horse would stand shaking once he had stopped. If we had a chance, we stroked him and talked to him quietly, and I think he got comfort from it.

When the horses finished work, they were unharnessed and brushed and turned out into the field. A bucketful of water was always given to them, but, after galloping round in sheer delight at being free, they always went over to the brook to see if there was water in it. If any water was in the brook, the bucket was ignored. They would far rather find their own water than drink from a bucket. Tom always rolled over and over for good measure while he was young enough.

The horses were all given titbits which they loved. These included apples, sugar lumps, biscuits and carrots. We had been forbidden to give them large pieces of bread. No reason was given for this ruling and we children thought it was just one more instance of the grown-ups wielding their power. This suspicion was fed by the fact that every day one of our customers gave Tom pieces of bread. He stopped at her gate and crossed the pavement and his head almost reached the window of her house across the tiny front garden. The lady would come out, bread in hand, and Tom would enjoy ten minutes of chewing and getting the bread past his bit. My sister and brother discussed this and reasoned that horses mouths were big and should be able to take large pieces. One day they secretly gave Old Tom several large slices of bread and noticed that he seemed to make a great deal of fuss eating them. The next day he ate nothing at all and we were all worried. He looked pathetic with his head hanging down and his whole body sagging. If father had sent for the vet, we really would have been in trouble, because when Naomi and Eric succeeded in getting Tom's mouth open, they saw what was wrong. The bread had stuck firmly across the roof of his mouth and had hardened and become a solid soggy mass, which prevented anything being eaten. They worked at it feverishly and finally cleared it. They were terrified they would be caught. Old Tom survived. He was a born survivor. We loved him for his kindness to us, his courage, his obstinacy, for just being there so that we could go to him and tell him our troubles. His ears would move forward and back and he would snuffle softly. We always felt better for telling Tom. We would always pretend we were grooming him.

Old Tom's life and ours were inextricably bound up together, and even when he became really old and his eyes were tired, his back sagged and his head often drooped, we never imagined life without him. He was retired and lived quietly, having his shed in the paddock, his bowl of oats each day, his water, hay if necessary and his occasional grooming.

My sister Naomi was engaged to the man who is now her husband at that time, and often in the summer evenings Naomi and Bert took Tom along the lane, where he stopped when he chose to pull the lush grass, and up on to Whaddon Green. There they would sit for a while to let him wander quietly round, eating a little here and there as he wished. He loved this and would watch for them to come to the paddock gate to fetch him, but eventually he became too old and weak to walk far. He was almost blind, although his hearing was still acute. He would whinny when he heard us coming to give him his morning bowl of oats and snuffle as he ate them.

One morning when I went to feed him, he was down on the floor. He made gallant attempts to get up, but was unable to do so. A great fear, the same dread that I have had several times during my life, possessed me. I went quickly back to the house and told them. That morning his life ended and part of our lives went with him. Our home was a very silent place for days afterwards. We never found a replacement for Old Tom.

Lady was a tall black thoroughbred, belonging to Mr Charlie Jones of Glencoe. Part of Lady's work was to pull a wagonette. She never went faster than a sedate trot and, while she was between the shafts of the wagonette, she always looked a lady. Her owner, Mr Charlie Jones, a corpulent man who sported a luxuriant moustache, used to sit on the front of the box, surveying the scenery and obviously enjoying riding behind Lady.

The wagonette was the first step in our village towards public transport;

Charlie used to take seven ladies into Gloucester to do their shopping. Some he took on Wednesdays and others on Saturdays, putting them down at a point near the town centre. He then took Lady to a quieter street and waited until his passengers were ready to return home after about two hours. This jaunt was rather in the nature of an outing to our village folk. The wagonette rolled slightly to Lady's leisurely trot and the village ladies, being elderly, rolled with it, gossiping and laughing, telling the latest scandals on the way. It usually occupied the whole morning, but time was less precious then and life was lived at a much quieter pace than it is today.

Lady was always well groomed and when she was pulling the wagonette, she looked a fine horse and trotted proudly. But the gentle mare had another job, which did not suit her half so well. She pulled a smallish trolley on several days each week, because Mr Charlie Jones was the village coalman, as well as private hire man. On these days, she lost all her proud bearing and positively drooped.

There came a time when Charlie had great difficulty in getting the coal trolley out of his drive and on to the road. His entrance was next to a farmer's field and for years the farmer firmly refused to cut his hedges. They were of hawthorn and contained a treasure house of blackberries, watched eagerly as the berries ripened to be picked for jam, but they overhung Charlie's drive so much that there was scarcely room for the trolley to pass. After a lot of fuss and bother, the farmer was obliged to cut his hedges — much to the relief of Lady and her driver. Their joy was short-lived, however. There is an odd country law which says that if you own a hedge and there is a ditch beyond it, you are responsible for the upkeep of the ditch. The farmer suddenly remembered his duty, and cleaned out the ditch, deep and wide — Charlie, Lady and trolley had an even harder task now. The laden trolley had not room to pass up the drive without the wheels falling into the well-dug ditch. Charlie remonstrated, but his old enemy just stood his side of the hedge and laughed, which infuriated Charlie. When his arguments failed to get any response, he took the farmer to court.

Everyone in the village took sides, and we all read *The Citizen* excitedly each evening, to see what the previous day's proceedings had turned up. The case went on for some days and eventually we learned that Charlie had won. The ditch had to be piped in, which cost the farmer quite a lot of money. Charlie had sued for damages and these he got — one farthing! Lady was the only one to gain, and least she could come and go without having to wait while a trolley was unloaded so that it could be pulled free!

Few people had horses for pleasure alone. Our Doctor used a horse and trap for years, and there was no such thing as reaching an urgent case in a short time. First the patient's relative or friend had to reach the Doctor (a journey of over two miles), before the advent of telephones. Next, the Doctor's horse had to be harnessed, unless it and the Doctor were already out on another case. If it was dark, there were only paraffin carriage lamps, which did not light up the dark lanes very well. Doctor and horse reached their destination just as quickly as was possible.

When motor transport came, Dr St Johnson had one of the first motor cars we saw. It had a low ridged bonnet and the body was very high and had a fretted rack on top to carry luggage. The upholstery was of beautifully buttoned leather. The car could travel at all of twenty miles an hour, so Dr St Johnson and his patients were able to get together more quickly than before.

The Sinnott family acquired a little black mare and a black and red trap, which everyone thought very smart. Queenie was a high stepper, full of the joys of spring. Their gardener, Mr Merriman, found a new lease of life. He was now required to act as coachman, which changed his restricted life greatly. He really enjoyed ferrying the young people about. Later Queenie was exchanged for Topper, who was much more staid, with a trap which was brown and not considered nearly so exciting. The cars which came later on gave us all greater speed, but much less fun.

Chapter Six   Farming and a Farm

Our village was surrounded by farms. There were four, including Tuffley Court, which bordered our lanes.

Between 1920 and the late 1930s, times were hard for farmers and those who made their living on, or from, the land. During the 1914-18 War, farmers had been urged to grow more grain, livestock, vegetables and fruit, but after the Armistice, when so many people found themselves unemployed, where they had access to a little land, they produced all the chickens, eggs and vegetables they could. Suddenly, partly through other countries dumping their produce on our markets, and partly because unemployment and low wages did not allow people to buy all they could have consumed, we found there was a glut of most things. Vegetables, fruit, meat, grain and milk had to be sold at prices too cheap to be economic, and at that time there was no help from the Government.

People, generally, were poor, and continued to be so throughout the 1920s and 1930s. This, for farmers, meant that very little improvement would be carried out; they turned to dairying rather than cropping their land; herds deteriorated because of the lack of money for foodstuffs and replacements, and the shabbiness of farms and smallholdings all over the country reflected the difficulties in which their owners found themselves.

As little labour as possible was employed, while machinery, which has now cut out the work of so many men, was not yet in a greatly advanced stage. Fields went rough and were left undrained; farm buildings became even more run-down than four years of war had left them; hedges went wild and the owners could not spare the labour to lay them. It was a vicious circle: the less money invested on improvements, the less the farm produced and the less money was made.

Prices remained low because people generally had not enough money to pay more, and food was continually wasted. Farmers often fed crops to stock, rather than pay for their cartage to markets where they would be sold at prices which would not offset the costs incurred. During the General Strike, my father sold cabbages at a penny each — no one could afford more.

Until World War II, producing food was hard and unrewarding, then, when the farmers were once more required to improve their production, science gave all available help and subsidies made improvement possible. Prices rose again and once more growing food became profitable. The War Agricultural Executive Committee turned every stone to see that farmers got a better deal.

The industry has never looked back, though for a long time, growers, having been let down for so many years, were far from eager to do all the things they were suddenly required to perform, such as ploughing more land, cleaning out thistles and docks, adding manure and artificial fertilizers to improve the soil, setting potatoes and wheat, increasing the value of their herds and weeding out poor stock. For many people it meant a completely different way of doing things, but gradually standards and prices rose until the industry was once more important and production increased a hundredfold.

We naturally knew more about the working of the farm we dealt with and its fortunes and misfortunes affected us as well as the owners. Cows and their products were literally our bread and butter; if anything untoward happened to even one of the herd, the trouble was reflected immediately in loss of milk. For many years most of our milk came from Tuffley Farm, which was then owned by a Mr Savage. During the 1920s and 1930s, the cows were hand milked. The warm milk was strained, then taken and sold right away. Later, we installed a cooler to reduce its temperature. Cold water ran through the centre of the cooler, while the milk ran down the outside and was cold by the time it reached the bottom and ran into the churn. It was fascinating to watch the milk rippling down the corrugated cooler. Gradually farms were required to cool their own milk and eventually cows were machine milked in a proper milk parlour; the milk was cooled and then sent by tanker — instead of the traditional churns — to the nearest large dairy in the neighbourhood, where it was sterilized and sold. The process improved until, nowadays, tankers are used for transporting most of the country's milk, and it is sterilized and bottled at its receiving depot. The smaller dairies have, with some exceptions, all been bought up by a few large depots and there are fears that the actual farms will soon be acquired by large combines or co-operatives, until no small farms, or only a very occasional one, remain.

Until World War II, the price to be paid by the dairyman to the farmer for milk was agreed by the local Dairymen's Association and it was frequently left undecided until the day before the change took place. Settlements were made at half-yearly intervals, with cheaper rates in the summer, when milk is more plentiful, and dearer prices in winter, when the extra cost of additional feeding was more expensive, and milk in shorter supply. Farmers must find it easier now that an overall price is decided on for the whole country some time before it becomes fact. Life was much more unsettled in those days, but people were allowed to remain individual.

Parts of the farmhouse and buildings at Tuffley Farm were very old. There was an enormous granary below a loft where roots, grain and beans were stored. This building, of brick, had large double doors at both front and back, so that a loaded waggon could be driven in at the back and unloaded. It was then taken out by the front doors and the horses had no need to turn.

The tallot was another well-built unit, where horses could be stabled on the ground floor. Upstairs hay and straw were stored. The steps up to the loft were of stone, and built outside the building. The cow byres were always reasonably clean, but needed to have money spent on them.

The inside of the house was fascinating. A large, stone-floored kitchen, with a huge settle, was the meeting place for everyone who came and went. A range was always alight and I have seen a whole salmon cooking, wrapped in buttered greaseproof in the fish-kettle above it. Like many old farms, it used to have its own peculiar smell; so many sides of bacon had been cured in the kitchen, so much milk and cheese and butter were stored in the dairy which adjoined the house and was another stone-floored building. In the old days, the parlours were rarely aired and I remember an evening of card-playing when we were quite young, the room lit by an oil lamp and filled with all the Victoriana which is so much sought after today. For many years nothing seemed to change, and the room smelled as most parlours did.

Then we suddenly heard that the Savage family were to leave Tuffley Farm and it was taken by a progressive businessman named King. He had the necessary cash to make many improvements and began by enlarging the farmhouse. Gradually the byres were cemented and brought up-to-date; the yard was cemented and the pond filled in. These ponds accumulated a whole collection of items. Ducks are always kept in their houses for part of the morning, because they are notorious for laying their eggs in the pond. Rubbish lying around is liable to be thrown in, out of sight. Quantities of both were found when that pond was cleaned out.

We loved to wander round the buildings to watch what was going on. Twice each day the cows were hand milked. In the spring the sheep-shearers would come, and they reckoned to take off a fleece without breaking it, in, it seemed, an incredibly short time; the fleece was then rolled up and stacked.

Threshing was done in the autumn. The machine, accompanied by the van in which the men who worked it lived, visited most of the local farms and the men worked like demons to get the work done and pass on to the next customer. They even worked in the dark and it fascinated us to watch through the big barn with the two sets of double doors as the fire, which drove the steam engine, roared away. The scuttling men looked like black devils as they pitch-forked the sheaves on to the monster's elevator. Sparks and chaff flew everywhere and the men's faces, blackened by dust and soot, were streaked with channels where the sweat had run down.

Geese were kept at Tuffley farm. The Chinese keep them as watchdogs; they performed the same service at the farm. It was not really safe to venture in at the gate while they were in the yard. They paddled towards one on their great flat feet, waving their wings and stretching out their necks, screeching and hissing. They could use their wings as weapons and gave a person a heavy blow, if they wanted to. None could go past the farm gate without those geese knowing it and setting up a commotion which warned the people inside the house.

At Whitcombe Farm, Guinea fowl (which we called gleanies) were the custodians. They, like the geese set up their peculiar calls directly anyone approached. As the dogs were so often on duty elsewhere, it was necessary to have some sort of alarm.

Farmer King was a dealer, rather than just a producer of milk or an arable farmer. He bought animals, kept them for a time, then sold again, and he had prospered. He seemed to have second sight or an instinct which told him what to buy and when to sell. This enabled him to make the improvements which, in turn, caused the land to produce more. When he came to the farm, everything changed. The farm labourers who had worked there for so long had to decide whether they could continue to work for a new master, who had progressive ideas and who introduced machinery which needed people skilled at working it. Some of them chose to leave their tied cottages and the job they had known for many years, to begin afresh somewhere else.

Tractors and a lorry to carry livestock replaced some of the horse-drawn vehicles, and the whole place was made tidy. Barbed wire lined all the hedges, some of which were laid for the first time for years. It is true that a few milking cows were kept, but most of the stock was bought and sold fairly quickly.

Then one unforgettable autumn, disaster struck. The disease which every farmer dreads—foot and mouth—appeared among his stock. To have this happen is a traumatic experience for any farmer. Perhaps only one animal will start limping and saliva will run from its mouth. These symptoms are caused by blisters. The cow, which was perfectly healthy until that day, stops feeding, does not remain with the herd, but stands dejectedly alone. The farmer must call the vet at once, and just occasionally the illness proves to be something different from foot and mouth. If the disease is confirmed, then the whole herd of cattle, all the pigs, everything with cloven hoof, must be slaughtered. The illness is not fatal, but infected herds can spread the disease very quickly until no herd in the country is free. Foot and mouth disease is carried by foxes, rabbits, birds, rats—all the smaller animals—so immediate action is necessary. Vaccines are used today at all surrounding farms in an effort to stop an outbreak from spreading, but there are many different types of this disease and no one vaccine can cope with all of them, so that success is not always assured.

I remember, when I was very young, listening to my father and another farmer talking about it. They said that in their young days people cured their cows by making them walk through gateways spread with quicklime. This must have been cruelly painful, even if it effected a cure. They also painted the animals' hooves with Stockholm tar. Stockholm tar is still a very highly valued disinfectant.

At the time we experienced foot and mouth disease in our supplies of milk, there was only one cure—every cloven-hoofed animal on the farm had to be killed, until nothing was left which could spread it. No one from outside the farm, except the vet and an assistant, was allowed in. These two had to wash their gumboots in disinfectant before leaving. Gradually the lowing herd became silent, the whole animal life was wiped out. The shooting continued remorselessly; the long barrows filled with quicklime grew longer and longer. The farm, which so recently had been a busy, sometimes noisy, place, became literally as silent as the grave. The stench of death, burning and disinfectant pervaded the lane and surrounding fields.

The farmer and his family were isolated and a stunned sense of shock took over not only them, but the whole of our small community—cut off and unable to help. There is no comfort for a family that has seen the results of years of work and care wiped out in a day or two, and yet Tuffley Farm was less badly hit than some farms where pedigree stock was infected. Mr Webb of Hardwicke lost his herd of Gloucesters (chocolate brown, with a white streak down the centre back and a white tail). This herd must have taken years of patient work to build—breeding, discarding the imperfect animals, having a vet to test them regularly and to advise. Many thousands of pounds, as well as a lifetime's effort had gone in a few days. Insurance cannot compensate for this kind of loss.

In Mr King's case, as soon as they recovered from the first shock, he set about rebuilding his life. For us, the outbreak meant finding another farm to supply our milk—a nightmare situation in itself. It was eventually achieved and the Model dairy let us have a quota to tide us over.

The farm was a wonderful place for children to play and we often joined the King youngsters for an evening's fun. There was a tennis court where we learned the game and occasionally we were allowed to ride the horses. We were expected to teach them to jump, but I was never successful. When I rode the horse, he always refused to jump. He knew I was soft! One evening, when we had been riding the little horse too hard and he was hot and bothered, Mr King came home and caught us. He was furious—and rightly so—and made us walk the horse round until he was cool again.

Apart from tennis and riding, hide and seek was our favourite game. The tallot, where the hay and straw were kept, the feeding bins and the great barn, where grain was brought and stored before threshing, contained many wonderful hideouts and often the finder was beaten. We would burrow deep into the Indian corn vats or among the locust beans. Sometimes the finder got tired of looking and we had to play another game.

Mr King had four daughters but only one son. Percy was a smaller edition of his father. He had little use for school lessons and stayed away to work on the farm whenever he could find an excuse to do so. Gloucester cattle market was held on Mondays and that day Percy was always absent. Dad said, 'Well, he'll learn more at the market than he would at school'. While this was debatable, Percy certainly learned what it meant to buy and sell stock while he was young. By the time he was eleven years old, and when money was worth many times as much as it is today, he would go to market, taking his animals, which he had bought, kept and fed, sell them and come home in the afternoon with fresh stock and £20 in his pocket. He was allowed to buy what he could afford on his own account and take it home, and his father would let him use the farm foodstuffs and either a field or pen, depending on whether he bought cows, sheep or pigs, and they were Percy's responsibility. He had to feed them, get the vet if necessary, water them and care for them until he thought they were the right size and in the right condition to be sold. When he sold them, at his own judgement, the money they brought was his. He was allowed and encouraged to think for himself, his father provided food and accommodation. Percy was rich before he left school.

Farmers' wives and daughters worked very hard both inside the houses and on the land, but we were all conscious that farming was men's business; they did the managing and made all the decisions. Most wives claimed the money earned for selling their eggs as their perks.

Winter brought the hunt to the farm lands. The hunt rarely caught a fox, but we were always thrilled by the sight of horses and riders, well groomed and turned out, the members usually in pink, but many followers in hacking jackets and breeches or jodphurs on horses which ranged from hunters, to hacks, to ponies. Some of the ponies unashamedly refused to jump the hedges and had to be led through the gates, some followed round the lanes, and it was quite a common thing to be asked which way the hunt had gone. The hounds were always eager and we couldn't help getting excited as we watched them, followed by the horses, streaming out over the meadows, and heard the huntsman's horn as he gave various signals.

I think that in our youth we only appreciated the sense of urgency, colour and the spectacle of the hunt; we never thought of the cruelty which might be involved. Many people on bicycles and in cars also followed the hunt, but they had to stick to the lanes through which they travelled at a furious pace, dangerous to themselves and any other user of the road. They would often shout and ask us which way the hunt had gone; if we knew, we told them.

One morning, as we were walking with mother in Grange Road, a horse and rider passed us and called out something which sounded like, 'Did you back Dry Toast?' This seemed double Dutch to us and, after pondering for a while, we gave up working on it. We had expected an enquiry about the hunt and he had gone before we realised that this was not such a query. It was only much later in the day, when we heard that Dry Toast was the name of that year's Derby winner, that we guessed that he must have had something to do with the horse.

The hunt rarely gave up their chase until either they caught their quarry or the darkening sky of evening made cross-country riding too dangerous to continue. Then they would straggle home in small groups through the muddy fields in the gathering dusk, tired and thinking only of unharnessing their mounts and stabling them before enjoying a bath and change and a hot meal.

On one such winter evening, the fox had his revenge. Everyone who had been out hunting was too tired to even think of shutting up the chicken house. At Tuffley Farm the chicken house was in one of the home fields. The birds were all inside, but the outer shutter was not closed. Reynard got inside and in absolute silence killed all of them—two dozen laying hens. The hatred the farmers hold for the fox is not so much because he will kill and take just what he—or she—needs, but because, either for greed or as a cache of food to come back to for feeding cubs, or just in wantonness, the animal will kill every bird or small animal he can reach. Cats are not immune and our own cat has been cornered by a fox once or twice while out after dark.

Possibly the fox or vixen think they are laying up store for the cubs, but people in the country who leave their fowl houses open at night do so at their peril. No hens were spared at Tuffley Farm on that occasion and there were many cheap chickens in Lower Tuffley next day for those who wanted them.

The farmers who had been at the hunt and their workmen took turns at watching with a gun at the ready every night for the following week, hoping that Reynard would return, but either he caught their scent or had other prey to catch, for he never returned to the scene of the crime.

Farmer King's alterations and improvements at the farm continued from year to year. We had been used to seeing tree-lined lanes and heavy topped hedges, trailing hops or dog roses or bryony, but we had to learn that timber was there to be felled, as soon as it reached maturity, and hedges would be laid and all the lovely wild briars, which had rooted themselves, would be ruthlessly cut out. The elm trees which studded the hedges had been growing for years, and we knew each familiar shape.

One autumn the woodmen came marking with a splash of whitewash those which were to be felled that winter. We dreaded seeing the trees come down, because we loved our lanes just as they were and, treeless, they would be barren places.

There were perks, though. The woodmen let anyone who wanted to do so take the smaller branches, the rotten pieces and the chips they cut from the base of the tree, because these were not of use for selling and would have to be cleared in any case. Dried they made good firewood and all the village children went out after school and at weekends 'wooding'. It was hard work, but it helped our fuel supply and we never went home empty handed, but either dragged a limb behind us or carried a sack of chips. Dad often bought a cord of wood to be cut into logs with a circular saw later on. A cord consists of logs from four or five inches thick to about eight or ten inches. They are nearly a yard long and are stacked between upright posts of the same wood, the whole structure containing about 128 cubic feet of wood. There was fun and hard work loading the cart and unloading it at home, and further work when the circular saw and its engine were brought in to reduce the logs to a reasonable size for chopping, ready for firewood. The dried logs gave scented fires all through the following winter. Most of the village benefitted from tree-felling, though none of us liked the resulting gaps in the hedges where the lovely elms had once stood.

The woodmen were very strict about letting any of us go anywhere near a tree they were preparing to fell, because of the danger involved. The tree would be standing one minute and falling the next. The elms gave no warning when they were about to fall, but with a shudder and a dreadful groan would sweep down and measure their length on the grass below in a matter of seconds.

There were no mechanical saws for felling trees at that time; the woodmen, having cut a wedge-shaped piece from the bottom of the trunk with their axes, used a long cross-cut saw to cut through the remainder of it. The weight of the top brought the tree down. The men always knew exactly when and where it would fall.

This part of the general cleaning and clearing of his property often brought Mr King along to watch the proceedings. He was always warned, as we all were, but one day his interest made him late in responding to the cry 'TIMBER'. The tree fell too swiftly for him to get clear and the top branches caught him, causing injuries from which he died a few days later.

This tragic happening shocked the whole village. It seemed impossible that such an active, progressive personality should have vanished from the scene. People wondered how his projects could continue, but the training given to his son at an early age enabled him to take the reins and his experience served him well.

Chapter Seven   Post-War Years

As my father had chosen to return to Dairying when he came home from the army, he needed to buy back his business from Mr Savage, who was then at Tuffley Farm, and to accomplish this he had to work for some years for very little money, the rest of his wages being accumulated until he had repaid the buying price. Mother still helped to work the smallholding to make up enough for us all to live on.

Everyone had to help to regain our independence and each of us children had to do a certain amount of work each morning before school, as well as in the evenings and at weekends. One of us went on the milk-round with dad, while the other two helped at home. We changed jobs each week in rotation. At home our chores included washing and drying the breakfast dishes, watering the livestock and helping to feed them when we were old enough to be reliable; we also had to pump up water to fill a 150 gallon tank in the orchard, which supplied the needs of the house and for washing the milk utensils. The tank required many more than 150 pumps, particularly when it was a dry summer. Two of us usually took turns at pumping. 'Pumping up the tank' was a common task for youngsters in the 1920s and 1930s. The well which supplied our water was very deep and, even in dry summers, rarely ran dry.

In the evenings, after washing and drying up the tea things, we sometimes groomed the horses, collected eggs and shut up the hen houses for the night. We all worked the whole of Saturday morning. My sister and I took it in turns to scrub the dairy. We also cleaned the knives and candlesticks, if we were not working on the milk-round. The dairy floor was made of white stone slabs of varying sizes and a wide granite shelf ran across one end. When it was finished and clean, the dairy looked and felt cool and lovely, but scrubbing it was very hard work. Candlesticks were later replaced by gas, and steel knives were superseded by stainless ones, which needed no extra cleaning after washing, and both improvements lightened labour.

The first house we served on our milk-round was, of course, the Grange. Here we often became involved in long and interesting conversations with Colonel Sinnott's daughters. When this happened, we completely forgot the time, then the unfortunate one on duty had to run a long way to catch up with the float and dad would be annoyed.

We had an alibi in the shape of a Brussels griffon. He was the Sinnott's tiny brown-haired dog, a parcel of bristling antagonism. He had large, protruding black eyes and a ruff of hair stood out all round his face and under his chin. He was a wonderful guard dog and his strategy consisted of hiding under the bushes which bordered the drive, until an intruder had passed, then darting out and nipping his or her ankle. While this did actually happen to us occasionally, it did not occur nearly as often as was claimed; but when talking made us late, we always blamed the dog. Father spoilt it all by going to see Colonel Sinnott about the dog and subsequently he was kept inside until after we had called with the milk. I only tried the alibi once more, but was caught out and none of us thought it worth trying again! Our morning talks ended too, as the girls were not allowed to delay us.

Talking, instead of working, made us late for school. Children under twelve years of age were not supposed to work before school, though this rule was less strictly observed in those days than it is now, when no children under fourteen are allowed to earn money for work before school. The schoolmaster came to our house to complain about this state of affairs, but the complaints only resulted in our having to get up slightly earlier and hurry a little more.

Life was not entirely filled with work and, although most youngsters during my childhood days worked more than they do now, life also held a great deal of fun and happiness. We always received wages for our work — one penny a day and sixpence at the end of the week. Our pennies were made to stretch as far as possible and with great cunning we were able to buy four different kinds of sweets. At Tuffley Post Office one could get sixteen raspberry drops, six love hearts, a length of liquorice or a liquorice pipe, and a gob stopper — all for a penny when first we began shopping. Even in those years the spending power of money decreased steadily, until one could only buy two different kinds of sweets for a penny. Small bars of chocolate ranged according to size from ½d to 2d each. Raspberry drops were good value and lasted a long time; love hearts had fond messages printed on them, they were usually shared for the fun of seeing what message the recipient got. Liquorice was not so exciting, but gob stoppers — well, they really lived up to their name. All children sucked them in school — chiefly because they were forbidden — and to do so was dangerous. Teachers had a habit of advancing with a piece of paper in one hand, and often without a word being spoken the gob stopper was given up and landed in the waste paper basket. They were popular because they were so large that they completely filled one's mouth or cheek. It was impossible to talk while sucking one; they were made of different coloured layers of icing and it was always exciting to take one out and see what colour had been reached, from time to time.

Between the wars, so many people took up pig and poultry keeping that they became unprofitable occupations; when pigs were sold, they often fetched less money than their food had cost, and a glut of eggs and chickens made them almost unsaleable. All through the village, people kept only as many pigs and poultry as they needed for home use and many pigstys and fowl houses stood empty. Children were always opportunists and soon made use of these empty houses. The boys took up pigeon breeding and Alban Cole, my brother's friend, actually worked his racing and homing pigeons. While not all the boys were so enterprising, many took up the hobby, keeping birds which produced their pigeon pairs of squabs frequently and regularly, becoming a menace to local gardeners. Most of the boys tired of this hobby in the end; corn was expensive for one thing and the bird houses required a lot of cleaning out, but Alban kept his pigeons for years.

The girls made houses for themselves wherever they could find an empty chicken house, though some of them became tool sheds. Two of our friends, Elsie and Gladys Oakey, had an old carriage for their 'house'. It was double seated, with a solid top and windows, and was painted black and yellow. It held four people and made a private retreat for youngsters when it rained.

My sister, brother and I had an unused hen house within its own run; the ground inside its enclosing wire fence had been well manured and made a fine garden where we grew beans, potatoes, peas and cabbage. We whitewashed the house inside, put up net curtains and covered the floor with old mats. Butter boxes made seats and we were given an old table. The nest boxes made good storage space and a couple of pictures on the walls completed the furnishings. We spent many happy hours there, sometimes with friends, sometimes by ourselves. The village girls visited each other's houses and a great time was had by all. Meals were often consumed in our retreats and we were given all the old china to use.

An exciting game we played each year, when the hay was made into a rick under the Dutch barn, was sliding down its sides from the top to the bottom. This lasted just until the grown-ups found out, and then the game ended abruptly.

This hayrick was a great attraction for a pair of pet Dutch rabbits. They often ran loose in the orchard and, if they were not watched, they indulged their mania for burrowing underneath it. Someone had to burrow in after them to get them out and great care was taken to conceal the mess made by these boring activities. People tended to finish up with eyes and hair full of hayseeds.

We were very lucky when we were young to have so much space in which to play. Other people often shared it with us. On wet days there was a great choice of places to play in. Besides having our hen house, we could climb up into the loft, which was a large space above our grain and fuel shed. The loft generally contained bales of hay, which made seats for several people. It was reached by climbing up an absolutely upright ladder, which was fixed and, therefore, could not be taken away. Often there were kittens in the hay, for Ruff, an old mother cat, always chose a bed of sweet smelling hay, in a fairly inaccessible place. She kept her kittens in the loft until she thought they were big enough to crawl, and then she brought them down to the house, one by one. No matter how many times the kittens were put back in the loft, once Ruff considered they were large enough for the house, she would take them down again, holding each one by the scruff of its neck and threading her way under and over the runs of the dangerous ladder. She always got her way in the end.

We did a great deal of French knitting there. We used cotton reels which had four nails hammered into one end, making a square. Wool was tied on to one nail loosely and wound round each other nail in turn; after that one just wound the wool round nails once and slipped the row of stitches, formed previously, over the new row. We used rainbow coloured wool and pulled the loose end down through the reel. It was always exciting when the knitting was finally long enough to appear at the bottom of the reel. I don't remember ever using the lengths of French knitting for any practical purpose, but everyone measured their knitting to see who had made the longest strip.

The loft was a wonderful place in which to hide, when there were jobs waiting to be done in the house. If we were all quiet, the grown-ups generally gave up listening to find out if we were there; then they went back to do the work themselves. If they had gone to the hen house to look for us, they would have got their feet very wet, as it was quite a long way away, through the orchard grass.

We kept a book there called *Guide to Scientific Knowledge of Things Familiar*, written by the Rev. E. Cobham Brewer. The title was always shortened to *Guide to Knowledge*. One of our number would ask us questions in turn and we tried to give the answers set out in the book; anyone failing to do so was 'out'—last man 'in' won and asked the questions next time. This was good fun for a while, but eventually everyone had learned the answers and the book lost its entertainment value.

The 'long-back-room' was another wet day rendezvous. It was a room which ran along the back of the house. Here the boys made weird machines with Meccano, until their supply of nuts and bolts ran out. One of these efforts was a crane, with a hook on the end of a length of string on a pulley. The string was let down from the landing by winding a handle, catching unwary people as they climbed the stairs, until the boys were made to stop it. People disliked having their hair pulled!

Another forbidden thing was a rope, tied across the room, attached to the door knob at one end and the catch of the window opposite at the other. We jumped over this until someone got caught in the rope, fell over backwards, and knocked herself out!

Two palliasses made a good base for budding gymnasts, and quite a lot of fun was had with them.

We all played tricks on each other. My sister was given a nurse's outfit for her birthday. It contained a syringe. I often had earache, which she decided to 'cure'. She filled the ear with water and I had earache for a week! Syringe confiscated.

Her own turn came in due course. Our schoolmaster, Mr Benjamin John Herrin, was a Methodist minister in his spare time. He had great faith—faith that children who had let him down time after time would one day justify his belief in them. Later on many of our schoolmates did so. On one occasion, he went a bit too far. He said that if only we had the necessary faith, we could do anything—if we wanted to, we could fly—if only we had faith. Later at home several of us discussed this and we decided to try it. I am not sure whether it was by a process of elimination, but somehow Naomi was chosen as the guinea pig. We all willingly helped her up on to the ridge of the pigsty roof, about eight foot above the ground and persuaded her to jump off. Poor child, her faith and ours must have been very imperfect—she hit the floor with a sickening thud. Thanks to the long grass which softened her fall, she only suffered bruises, but she became very suspicious of games which gave her the star part after that.

My brother, Eric, might have been killed in a trick we played on him. All the village children hated pig-killing days; partly because the pigs always squealed so much, making us feel awful as we remembered them as we last saw them, partly because at those times the grown-ups all wanted to get the children out of the way.

The butcher travelled round the village in the autumn, which was a good time for pork, because the weather became colder and the meat kept fresher longer. No one then had a refrigerator. Some very privileged people had ice boxes, but only a few. Each family took their turn, so pig squealing was a feature of the village for some weeks. The butcher was good at his work and his knife was sharp and sure, so that death was instantaneous, and the squealing due to terror.

Some of the meat and offal was sold, but after a pig had been killed, everyone seemed to eat liver, faggots, chitterlings and brawn for a very long time. The leg would be sold or roasted; the pig's head made brawn and if the sides were not sold then they were salted down for bacon. They lay in salt for some days, after which they would be dried and hung in the kitchen to cure. The bacon from the sides kept good and lasted all the winter. Home cured bacon had a special aroma.

While a pig was being killed and dressed, we never seemed able to find the right place to go or a satisfactory game to play. Occupations are interesting enough when the people concerned choose them, but when we had to busy ourselves, there was always great difficulty in concentrating on anything but the one thing which was forbidden.

On one occasion we were given an old push-chair to play with. It was an Edwardian affair, made of American cloth encased in bent scroll-work. It had two small wheels at the front and two large ones behind. The rider was quite high off the ground. On this pig killing day my brother was strapped into this push-chair at the top of our steep drive and it was given a hefty shove. It hurtled down, out through the gateway, across the road, and overturned in a very prickly hedge. Eric was underneath it. Fortunately, he suffered only scratches and bruises, but the push-chair was confiscated and for some time after that we had to find some other amusement on pig killing days.

Pigs were a very mixed blessing. When a sow had too many piglets the runts (the smallest pigs) were given to the women and children to rear. For some weeks they were fed on milk from bottles and the men considered that this was no job for them. The piglets were greedy, snapping little things; they seemed forever hungry and were always ready to nip our fingers. As ours grew larger, they progressed from a box near the kitchen fire to a coop and run outside. In time, when they grew too large for their little houses, they were put into a hen run with a coop to retire into at night. By this time they were able to feed themselves on milk and meal, and they slurped and slushed it up with gusto. The milk and meal were given to us in exchange for looking after the animals, though when they were sold they often made a higher price each than the 'good' pigs did, and the women and children had this money for 'perks'.

For pigs, growing larger meant becoming more belligerent. Sometimes they were really spiteful. When one of the people who fed them was in the orchard, they were liable to break through the wire of their run to get to the food bucket. They caused endless spillages and hours of work repairing the damage they did. It was always so restful for a time when they at last went to market — for a time, until the sow farrowed again.

Of all the outdoor occupations the village afforded, swinging was, perhaps, the most popular. Most village families had their garden swing. These all faced in different directions, so that views given by swinging high were varied, and if you got tired of your own, you went and played on someone else's swing. Swinging gave the opportunity to catch up with the current occupations of most of our neighbours. There were glimpses of trains on the nearby railway line, animals — we knew all about the goats, piglets, dogs and poultry owned by everyone in sight — and the people talking across the garden fences or working in their vegetable patches. Swinging gave all sorts of little pictures impossible to see at a lower level.

Most of our swings were home made. Dad made ours. It was really tall and we worked the seat until we went higher and higher and the rings which held the ropes jumped dangerously in their hooks. Everyone performed as many hair-raising stunts as possible on their swings and these were duly enlarged as we related them to each other. We all found infinite variety and excitement in the acrobatics which could be performed on a swing.

All the village children seemed to do the same things at the same time. On wet days the boys made kites. These needed two thin strips of wood, one about 2 foot and the other 1 foot long. They were tied together so that the centre of the shorter piece was about two-thirds of the way along the longer strip. The lengths of wood were very light and of equal thickness. Notches were cut in the ends of the wood and string was taken tightly round the outside ends of the wood to give the kite shape. Strong brown paper, cut a little larger than the frame was then either stitched or stuck around it. The tail consisted of a long price of string on which, at six inch intervals, rolled strips of newspaper (about six inches wide) were tied. Depending on the weight of the kite, the

My brother Eric kite flying on the edge of the Cotswold Hills not too far from home. On this occasion the kite is not one of the type mentioned in the text.

tail had to be longer or shorter. Trial and error were the methods used, but generally two or three yards of tail held the kite straight and on course. We bought as many balls of string as we could afford and rolled most of it round the centre of a round stick, leaving enough room at each side to hold the kite, which could pull really hard in a keen wind. Although kite making was simple, it had to be strong or the wind tore it and the kite somersaulted to the ground. Fearsome faces were painted or stuck on to the front, and the kite was ready to fly.

Most local amusements were partially or completely home-made. Striped tops were sold in our village shops for about 6d each. We made the whips at home from a strong stick and thin, strong string. Skipping ropes and handles came complete, but one pair of handles lasted for three or four lengths of rope, which wore through as it hit the ground. Hoops hung outside the toyshops in Gloucester in great bundles. They were usually made from two thicknesses of bent wood, though some of them were of iron. Bowling a hoop or skipping got us to school early.

Hopscotch was completely home-made. The framework was either chalked on the road or yard or any hard surface, or dust was swept up to make a rectangle. This was divided into six squares, which were numbered. The shapes of outlines varied a lot, the more odd the shape, the harder the game. All that was needed to play was a small tile or flat stone, which was slid along the floor to land in a square. We started from square one and progressed until each square had been played. One hopped all round, picking up the stone and taking it along. Sometimes a rest was made on one square, where both feet could be on the ground at the same time. Those who over-shot the square being played were out. Handicaps increased and one by one players had to drop out, leaving the last as winner.

We played marbles all the way home from school. We never dared to play on the way there, because that game always made us late.

When the roads were covered with tarmac and they should have been better for these pastimes, motor traffic increased until finally it was too dangerous to play outside the playground.

The boys all played football and cricket, of course; sometimes in the lanes but more often in one of the fields, where grass was not wanted for hay. We were quite poor in the 20s and 30s, but we made our own fun and it was time consuming and rewarding, and our play was utterly absorbing so that, while we may have worked harder than children do now life was full and interesting. Of course, in those days, children were much freer than it is possible for them to be now.

Different seasons seemed to produce games which we all played at the same time. Perhaps because we all want to be alike, everyone either played marbles, whipped tops, skipped, played hopscotch, ball, housekeeping or flew kites at the same times. After three weeks or a month of one occupation, we passed on to the next, all together. Children then did not, as a whole, seem to be as interested in making collections of things as they are now.

One female occupation for hot days was 'making scent'. For this we had a bottle and visited all our friends' homes begging a bloom here and another there, until our bottle was full. We then added water and if we thought the perfume was 'right', corked it down. It was then shaken every day until it looked as if it were finished. After a few days, the scent was opened and usually the result was — horrible. Instead of the interesting aroma, which was certainly there when the bottle was corked, a foul smell met our noses. We never seemed to learn, but 'made scent' year after year, always with the same result; we did not realise that to obtain good perfume, the essence of flowers must be distilled.

On fine sunny days, groups of children from Tuffley and Gloucester often climbed Robinswood Hill, and it was possible to meet people from all the surrounding districts there. This was a favourite kite-flying place, the wind was always keen on top. The top is known from its shape as 'The Camel's Hump', with two separate summits.

There are many hills called Robinswood. Ours was about a mile and a half from our lane. We were always conscious of its nearness. The hill filled quite a large part of the landscape, and was near enough for us to spend some of our free time on its steep and slippery slopes as well as taking part in school excursions to its summit.

School outings were always unexpectedly interesting because the teachers chose different routes from the well-known ones we usually followed when other friends were with us. It was as if our teachers knew (as I expect they did) the well frequented parts of the district around us and took pains to show us the more unusual aspects of the hill. We went up by round-about paths, which often started from a lane at the end of Whaddon Green. From here, as we climbed, we hunted for all sorts of flora and fauna. There were unusual flowers like the tiny 'Star of Bethlehem', and we went through woods that were strange to us. A class of thirty or forty children made too much noise to be able to glimpse many wild animals, though we might catch sight of an occasional white scut as a rabbit scurried away to safety.

There was no wild honeysuckle in our lanes, but here in the woods it climbed over many bushes and its scent was sweet and heady. Great drifts of bluebells carpeted the woodland floor during the spring, and may bloom added its white canopies and its perfume. Eventually we would leave the woods and scramble up the remaining banks to the summit. The view of Gloucester and all the surrounding countryside is magnificent from the Camel's Hump on a fine day. Usually on the way down we came to the reservoir which supplies Gloucester with water. In those days a shop nearby sold cold drinks—sparkling orange, lemon and raspberryade. It was so welcome on a hot thirsty day and we drank and rested before the homeward journey. There was always water from an ancient well for those who had no pocket money.

When the weather was damp, the Hill was a formidable hazard. The clay of which it is formed became very slippery and keeping a foothold was difficult. We enjoyed its hazards, as youngsters love slipping and sliding, but sometimes bad accidents happened on the slopes.

The Hill is known to have been inhabited in prehistoric times; finds of pottery and an arrowhead have turned up during digging operations. During the late 1800s, a brick and tile works existed at the foot of Robinswood. Many of the houses in Tuffley and Gloucester were built from the good quality red bricks made there. The works flourished during the early twentieth century, but in the 1930s bricks from other parts of the country were bought because they were cheaper. Motor transport made this possible. The kilns were always busy during the 20s and well into the 30s, but the works were finally closed in the early 40s. In its heyday many local men got their living at the brickworks and their houses had been built in roads adjacent to it. As work here gradually lessened, our village and Upper Tuffley were badly hit. Local men had to join the ranks of the unemployed at a time of great depression.

Small groups of us climbed the hill for many different reasons. There were thickets of blackberry and elder bushes. Many people used the berries for home-made wine and they paid us well for berries we collected. Groups worked all Saturday afternoons to fill baskets and pails with them. There was always great rivalry to see who gathered the most, though those who got the largest amounts did not always get the most money. Green berries, leaves and general bits and pieces reduced the price. Mushrooms were another bonus from the Hill, though luck had to be on one's side. Often people got up very early to find mushrooms, and stalks were all that was left of a ring later in the day. Our neighbours made ketchup with them, and we could earn sixpence for each pound we picked.

During the early part of the twentieth century, we still observed parts of ancient customs, although at the time we had no idea that the things we considered fun, had been handed down from prehistory. Robinswood is a beacon hill, so, of course, warnings of danger or celebrations have always taken the form of a huge fire, one of a circle round the Cotswolds. Even as late as the 1939 war, we knew that one of the signs of invasion would be the ring of fire round Gloucestershire. Thankfully, it was never needed for this purpose.

On Good Fridays, many of us took Hot Cross buns and drink up the Hill and consumed them on the Camel's Hump. At the time, we supposed our parents were glad to give them to us to keep us occupied on that day. We had no idea that we were enacting a small part of the pagan ceremony of the Spring equinox (the days on which the hours of light and darkness are equal). Hot Cross buns were made in the old days too, the quarters representing Spring, Summer, Autumn and Winter. The Christian religion adapted them for Good Friday, as it did many other ancient customs, so that people who were being asked to forsake heathen worship, might yet keep some continuity with the past.

Although we did not climb the Hill on Midsummer morning, we often got up very early to watch the sun rise behind it — so did our ancestors.

On Midsummer morning from our village, the sun made a halo round the top of the Hill as it rose. This also had some significance in prehistory.

Our hill remained as we remembered it all our young lives: an old friend we visited from time to time and loved always.

Chapter Eight   To Sir With Love

The two parishes of Tuffley and Whaddon always had strong associations. The school was based in Whaddon and St. Margaret's Church was at Whaddon, too. Children attended school from about 5 to 14 or 15 years of age. If one was lucky, admittance could be earlier than 5, and I began at about 4½ in 'the Infants' Room'.

The head teacher there was Mrs Brown. She always seemed old, although she could not have been more than 40 when I first knew her. She was fat and comfortable, with a blouse and skirt, over which she always wore an apron, tied tightly about her middle. She had grey hair, and steel rimmed spectacles, over which she surveyed us from her desk if we became noisy while she marked the register or corrected lessons. She always had more than 40 children to teach, with three separate grades—the 'babies', aged from about 4 years old; the second class, aged from 6 to 7, and the first class, who were seven and over. Pupils went into the Junior Department at around 8.

Mrs Brown kept strict discipline, with a long knitting needle always held on her desk, ready to deal with anyone who became obstreperous. We all respected her and stood in awe of her; she was very strict, but kind and fair as well.

The schoolchildren assembled in long lines in the playground five minutes before 9.0am, summoned by a clanging handbell or a piercing blast from a large whistle. Both could be heard a long way off, so there was no excuse for being late. Immediately before 9.0am, we filed into our lobbies and took off our outdoor clothes. The very young ones were helped by older children. Everyone went into classrooms in an orderly way — even the Infants — and remained standing, while Mrs Brown said 'Good morning, children', to which the answer, delivered in a sing-song manner, was 'Good morning, Mrs Brown'. Thereafter, we called her 'Teacher'.

Prayers were said while pupils stood at their desks, after which a glorious banging ensued, as desk seats were let down as noisily as possible. Sometimes we were severely admonished about this and made to 'do it again, more quietly this time, please'. But the joyful noise always returned after a few days. After the class was seated, the register was called and children answered, 'Yes, teacher', when present. There would be a silence if no one replied when their name was called and Mrs Brown surveyed us over her specs. The register was finally put inside her desk and work began in earnest.

There was no nonsense about 'learning by play'; we did play, hard and long, but lesson times were strictly for learning and even the babies began by writing letters and figures, later progressing to script and small sums. Very easy addition and subtraction started quite early; everyone did simple knitting and the top class, elementary sewing. It was a very busy day for small children and at 3 o'clock, when Mrs Brown saw to it that work was put away in the cupboard and she took out her book and settled the class so that she could read to us, the tinies were always ready to go to sleep.

'I remember, I remember' — her voice came and went in our drowsy minds, as we lay with our heads on our arms on the desk-tops and dozed. This was only allowed while we were in the Babies class; after that attention had to be given to the story or poem or else! Starting school was wonderful, because there was never enough for us to do at home and school was a whole new world. It was a very tiring world at first and the babies often finished the day asleep on their desk tops.

The department was always cosily warm, with a huge fire, over which a great black kettle steamed and sang, ready for playtime drinks for the teachers. Children were not supplied with milk in the 1920s. A guard surrounded the fire, which augmented two rows of pipes and large radiators in the winter. It was easy to drop off. Mrs Brown was a good reader. Some of her stories were exciting, some were the fairy tales we loved and learned so well it was easy to teach our own children about them. Poetry was more difficult, but although not always understood, the words flowed along and we learned a lot

Two views of the Whaddon Schools, taken from virtually the same spot. The top one is dated 1908 and clearly shows the wide grassy verge between the school railings and the Gloucester to Stroud road.

1979, the date of the second photograph, and the road is now a dual carriageway. Additional buildings have been connected to the main structure to cope with an influx of pupils, due to the building of several nearby housing estates since the Second World War.

of lines from such poems as Gray's *Elegy* and formed mind's eye pictures of the ploughman plodding home in the gathering dusk.

Our day began by singing, 'Every morning, the red sun', and ended with, 'Now the day is over', or 'Twinkle, twinkle, little star'. The Lord's Prayer was learned and repeated morning and evening, and stories from the Bible became familiar. At the end of the day came the Grace.

The Infants' room contained a huge cupboard, stuffed with an assortment of exciting things: pencils and paper, working boards, crayons — and something to remember always — a huge coloured basket-weave tin box, which held balls of plasticine. The smell when Mrs Brown opened the box was exciting and the models to be made were endless and fascinating. Knitting took a long time to learn and then, suddenly, the idea registered. Then everyone knitted long strips. Mine was pink and green and I was very proud of it — until a small schoolmate said scornfully, 'Pink and green, old maid's colours!' While not understanding what she meant, I still realised that Old Maid's Colours were something highly undesirable and knitting was continued only as a 'must' after that.

In addition to work and play at school for everyone, there were CELEBRATIONS.

Christmas was a wonderful celebration, and preparation began at least a month before we 'broke up' for the holiday. Dark afternoons, lamps lighted; making chains and lanterns in the Infant's room; more complicated things as one progressed through the school; Carols were learned; cards made; the Christmas story told and retold, and then acted; by the time end of term approached, the whole school was decorated. Occasionally the Vicar came for the final service.

One Christmastide, when the weather was dreadful, Mrs Brown took the whole department to her church at Tredworth, to see a Nativity Play. Afterwards, we all went to her home for tea. There we met Mr Brown. We were all most surprised to know there was a Mr Brown. During the 1920s, if women in Mrs Brown's social bracket had husbands, they did not work, they stayed at home. We learned, later, that Mr Brown was an invalid and Mrs Brown's salary kept both of them. Invalid or not, Mr Brown was a jolly soul, who seemed to enjoy vastly having a house full of eager 5 to 7 year olds, all talking at once, and he listened attentively to what was said about the play. I had never before been allowed to eat a meal away from the table, but with so many people crammed into the room, sitting was impossible. My friend Lilian says it was the first time she had ever eaten hundreds and thousands on her bread and butter.

No memory remains of going home; the afternoon's happenings filled everyone's mind to the exclusion of mundane things like a two-mile walk in the dark. There were no buses in Gloucester in those days, and the trams stopped more than a mile from Lower Tuffley.

The Easter lessons were taught very thoroughly and, while Good Friday always found us on holiday, with the school closed, it was one of the special days for everyone. We learned 'There is a green hill far away' for weeks beforehand, as well as at least one Easter hymn. The holiday, like Christmas, was full of meaning for the children. The significance of Whitsun, also, was taught thoroughly.

The first celebration I remember must have marked the end of World War I. The rain poured down all day and the lower school joined us in the Infants' room and shared our desks. There was tea with sandwiches and buns and drinks which we drank from the commemorative mugs which were given to each child. They had the heads of King George V and Queen Mary transferred on to them. They nearly all got broken with use later on; very few remained to be kept as mementos. It was a great occasion, though, and we sang lots of songs and played many games even in that confined space. I learned 'This Old Man' during the afternoon. The celebration ended with singing the National Anthem before prayers, after which school closed.

Of the secular celebrations, Empire Day was by far the most important and best loved. May 24th was a wonderful day. For weeks beforehand we practised singing 'Where the bee sucks, there suck I', 'Cherry ripe', and other old English songs. People who recited well said their pieces and, of course, we learned patriotic songs like 'Flag of Britain', a saga about the pageants and perils into which the Union Jack had got itself. Each chorus ended with 'We salute thee and we pray God to bless our land today'. The National Anthem had to be learned very thoroughly indeed and we practised singing it lined up, facing the flagstaff, for days beforehand; learning how to salute the flag. The idea of treating the flag with great respect was thoroughly instilled into us. As the actual day approached, the whole school gathered to itself an atmosphere of happiness and expectation.

On the Day, the folding glass and pine partition between two large classrooms was pushed back, making one really huge room. All the many windowsills of the very large windows were filled with red, white and blue flowers—peonies, lilac and iris. All the girls wore red, white and blue hair ribbons and clean dresses with white socks.

I never remember a wet Empire Day, there always seemed to be warm sun and a feeling of great happiness.

In the large classroom, after the flag had been saluted smartly, the children occupied half the space, while facing us were long rows of chairs on which the parents and other V.I.P.s sat. All would be there, including Colonels Jeune and Sinnott, with their wives and, sometimes, some of Colonel Sinnott's daughters, and always the vicar.

The arranged programme included songs, recitations and a talk, usually by one of the Colonels. Elizabeth Vowles reminded me of the occasion when the children had been drawing Union Jacks and had put them on to the wall upside down. Some had not grasped the fact that the white borders are not all the same width. It was Colonel Jeune's turn to talk and he delivered a severe lecture about the mistakes we had made. (The teachers must have been red-faced). He left us in no possible doubt as to the seriousness of our crime!

One incident which happened at this time stands out in my memory very clearly. My sister and I had been let out of school early to get some practice at home with mother — we were two of the children picked to sing 'Flag of Britain' — and, as we hurried along the lane towards the railway bridge, we heard the clop clop of cows' hooves, accompanied by a low mooing and the voice of the driver calling 'cup, cup'. It was the form of 'Come up', used in our district. The curve of the bridge hid the cattle from our view, so we were not able to tell how many there were, but we guessed they were mothers with calves. When the cows calved in the fields at night, they were brought up to the farm the next day. Cows having their babies with them are in no mood to be friendly; they have memories of being separated from their offspring and regard most people as enemies. Fear lent us wings. We sped back along the road until we reached a five-barred gate and climbed swiftly to the top, where it seemed safe. There were two cows, each with its offspring. Just as it seemed that they would pass by without incident, the nearest animal sighted us and made for the gate. She butted it with such force that my poor sister fell backwards on to the grass below. Naomi was always afraid of cows and this attack did nothing to alter her opinion of them.

Having unseated one onlooker, the cows took no further notice of us. The drover stopped to make sure that my sister was unharmed and the little herd plodded on towards the farm.

Whaddon School was very modern sixty years ago. It was an example of up-to-date planning and our Head, Mr Benjamin John Herrin, had every reason to be proud that he had been consulted when the plans were drawn up and had been able to introduce several ideas of his own. It was built to last; the rooms were large, light and airy. A garden was laid out in plots for the boys to cultivate, between the girls' playground and the lane. Twice a week, weather permitting, they went out, led by B.J.H. and dug or cultivated these plots. The produce was given to them as it matured; sometimes good and sometimes bad. Good when the girls could share green peas, bad when they were targets

Mr. B. J. Herrin, of 135 Tuffley-avenue, Gloucester, who was for 38 years headmaster of Whaddon Council School, has died at the age of 68.

He retired in 1943, and it was always his intention when he had the time to devote more of his energies to his church work and to take up local government work.

One of the greatest disappointments of his life was that his health was such that he was largely prevented from doing this.

He did contest the Tuffley Ward as an Independent in the 1945 municipal elections, and was beaten by a very narrow majority, but a serious illness which overtook him in the following year curtailed further activities in this direction.

He never fully recovered from that illness, but he was active until about a fortnight ago, when he was again taken ill, resulting in his death.

In his younger days he held a number of teaching appointments in Birmingham schools, and was appointed to his first headmastership at Horfield, Bristol, in 1903. After a short period at Nailsworth he was transferred to Whaddon in 1905 and remained there until the end of his career.

DEATH OF MR B. J. HERRIN

45 Years Local Preacher

He was actively associated with Tuffley Methodist Church and had preached at every one of the 100 odd Methodist churches around Gloucester.

For 45 years he was a local preacher and he travelled thousands of miles in neighbouring counties to do this work.

At Tuffley he had been Sunday school superintendent, choirmaster, treasurer to the trustees, circuit steward and president of the Adult Bible Class. He had been president and secretary of the Gloucester Sunday School Union and vice-president of the Gloucester and District Free Church Council.

Mr. Herrin had worked in several campaigns in the Stroud Division as a platform speaker for the Liberal Party, and in his younger days had been a referee for the Gloucester G.F.A. and helped to form a number of local soccer clubs.

He leaves a widow and two sons.

for the radishes the boys grew and threw.

While the gardening was in progress, the girls learned needlework. All very domesticated.

In the garden grew a very old pear tree, tall and laden with silver pears most summers. We were allowed three each when they were ripe — 'no more', said Ben Herrin, 'because no one can eat more than three'. (He probably thought about pear fights). The boys were sent up the tree to shake them down for us, and very good they were. The cores were thrown in all directions on the way home and our clothes rarely escaped staining.

At times, the Infants' room was used by the whole school. Those who stayed for dinner always ate their sandwiches there. Children provided their own drinks. The teachers always looked after us, sometimes eating their own sandwiches at the same time. No school lunches were provided until years later. The teachers always regarded supervising at lunch time as part of their duty and, after seeing that we cleared up our pieces and left the room tidy, they went out into the playground to join in games, unless the weather was wet.

Wet and cold days were wonderful, for then Mr Herrin returned to school early. If convenient, he came into the Infants' room, pushed out the old harmonium and played while everyone sang. We sang everything we knew. As more children returned to school, they came in and joined the singing. As often as not, a verse of a new hymn or song was included. One of the teachers would chalk up the words on the blackboard, while the tune was being learned. If the words were those of a new song, such as, 'Yes, we have no bananas', the children were encouraged to supply them, line by line. We were allowed to choose songs or hymns, one at a time, and we sang with all our might, until the windows became steamed up, so that we could not see out, and we got hopelessly flat. Then, whatever the weather outside, the large windows would be opened wide — and we continued singing.

Often the set lesson for the afternoon was forgotten as we sang or until it was time for play. We enjoyed these times so much and our teachers seemed to enjoy them too. Our Head was a very wise and kind person, although he could be strict, and he understood us all, and knew that we would learn better and more willingly if, occasionally, we were allowed to choose the lesson.

Girls and boys worked together, but on different sides of the classroom. We separated for games and went into either the girls' or boys' playgrounds — the infants, though, always joined the girls. The male teachers and Mr Herrin accompanied the boys, while two or three of the women teachers went with the girls. Both sexes played football in their separate areas; they were enormous, crazy games, involving everyone who wished to play. Pupils divided into 'sides' and one side played 'up' the playground and the other played 'down'. In the girls' area, one goal was the school gate and the other was the bicycle shed. The goal score was usually enormous (my side always seemed to lose) and we all went back to our lesson hot, out of breath and ready to settle down to work again.

Besides the rumbustious team games, which included rounders for the girls and cricket for the boys in summer, the girls all played ring games. There must have been a dozen of them: 'Big ship sails on the olly, olly, o', 'Poor Mary sits a-weeping', 'I sent a letter to my love', 'In and out the dusky bluebells', 'Oranges and lemons', and many others. We seemed to have new interests all the time.

The teachers supervised skipping, 'keeping the pot boiling' with from twelve to twenty girls, led by one who did something different each time round until ideas ran out or the rope caught her. There was also jumping, again in turn, each competitor dropping out as the rope went too high for her, until only the winner was left.

Early in the year, marbles was the rage and our teachers had a little peace while we all tried to win more marbles. Our marble bags were made during sewing lessons. Looking back, life at school evolved from our ideas, taken up and helped through by teachers who had never had to worry about psychology. Skills with hoops, single skipping ropes, and balls thrown at the school wall were encouraged. Provided blank walls were used and no windows were broken, no one stopped us. The school was strongly built of red brick, so we did no damage.

Children of all ages, from 5 to 15, played together on a surface scattered with small stones and, beyond a few bumps and bruises, no one was seriously hurt. From the time we started school, we were taught that older children looked after younger ones, and anyone foolish enough to disregard this rule would have had to face the mockery and ridicule of classmates, as well as a lecture from the teachers.

From time to time, our school was visited by various health officials. The District Nurse often came. She was nicknamed the 'Nit Nurse'. After looking us over critically, she parted our hair rather roughly in all directions. Many children had long hair which had to be kept plaited in school and we found it really difficult to straighten and replait after Nurse's ministrations. Anyone unfortunate enough to have acquired livestock was sent home and told not to return to school until there was not further risk of infection. Our spirits plummeted when we saw her wheeling her bicycle through the playground on her way into school.

The school Doctor was also accompanied by the Nurse. He was none too gentle and, after being weighed, people were examined very thoroughly and thumped on the back as he listened through his stethoscope. He needed to be thorough. In the 1920s, tuberculosis was rife and several of our schoolmates went down with it. The vaccine which controls T.B. had not been perfected then and hospital treatment was lengthy and uncomfortable. It was a disease which was treated with as much fresh air as possible and in winter this amounted to torture. People who returned cured could not stand the windows being closed and everyone had to get used to fresh air ad lib. in consequence.

The Dentist's treatment was Dickensian. His chair was reasonably modern for those days and tipped back, giving him a good view of his victims' molars. No such molly-coddling as stopping was entertained. If a tooth had a hole in it, he yanked it out, after spraying the gum to freeze it. No receptacle was kept for the extracted teeth, they were thrown on to the floor as they were taken out, and by the time he had seen a dozen patients there would be blood-covered teeth all over the place.

The Infants' department had been like one huge family, but 'going up' to the

Juniors was something of a shock. Mrs Brown had been strict and had stretched us fully, but she was essentially kind and understanding. In the Junior division, things were different. Textbooks were far more advanced than those we had been reading and, while they would have had a great attraction for older children, we found them heavy going. There were few pictures and the print was small. They would have been appreciated by much older children. *The Last of the Mohicans* was one example.

By now we no longer wrote 'script', but proper writing was expected to be done well. Drawing changed, and instead of using our imagination, we studiously and full of yawns copied 'still life'. This included cubes, oblongs, triangles, sometimes vases or fruit; drawing became a chore. Arithmetic was stepped up from adding and subtracting to multiplication, fractions and tables, including metric measures and weights. Tables were recited every day. As with spelling corrections, practice in repetition gave us a firm base on which to build, boring though it was.

The junior teachers were very strict, using the cane frequently on both boys and girls. We were caned for talking in class, for mistakes sometimes, and for badly written work. The teachers seemed to think that caning could supply the impetus to make us achieve more in less time. They did not appear to understand or care that their charges were being faced with work much too advanced for them. Perhaps they themselves were being driven to gain better results.

Two teachers particularly were guilty of this cruelty, and the severity of the punishment may be judged by the fact that one morning one of them accidently hit her own hand in mistake for a pupil's. She retired hastily, while another teacher continued her lesson. After play-break, she emerged from the library where she had taken refuge, red-eyed and with a swollen hand.

Our parents, especially mother, who had been a teacher of Juniors herself, determined to put a stop to this and when they found that complaining to the Head still did not have the desired effect, they put their complaint to the Board of Managers. This achieved their object and caning was cut drastically. Both these teachers left at the end of the summer term. Mr Herrin was often ill then, which may explain his non-intervention which puzzled us at the time.

In place of them, we got two jolly teachers — Miss Garraway and Miss Bick. They became firm friends with all of us and we noticed that new reading books and different sums were introduced. Although they knew how to control large classes, they helped us all, and in return we did our best for them, breaking out only occasionally.

Miss Bick, dressed in tweeds, woollen stockings and brogues, always rode a motor bike with sidecar. She gave off a very definite 'no nonsense' atmosphere. The motor bike was temperamental and often refused to start from the kick starter, so Miss Bick always had half-a-dozen hangers-on, waiting to give her a push. We would get up a good running pace and Miss B. would shove in the gear; the contraption leapt forward and some of us, inevitably, were left on the floor. We were lucky if we were only 'left standing'.

Miss Garraway, on the other hand, was tall and elegant. She had waved hair and always wore a string of pearls and either a long jumper or a fancy blouse, with which went silk stockings and court shoes. Her face was always well powdered. She was regarded as 'someone we would wish to grow up like' by the girls. Both teachers worked equally well with boys or girls, and we reacted accordingly.

This happy atmosphere continued until about a year before our class took the 11 + examination, or the scholarship as it was then known. At that point tragedy struck. Boss Herrin (always properly addressed as 'Sir' to his face), who supervised all his 11 + pupils very carefully, had a breakdown. We were like a ship without a captain and though we worked just as hard as usual, we were not guided in any particular direction and could not tell what progress we were making. The Head recovered and returned about a month before our exam, but we never caught up at this stage. Although I had always been a bookworm, my arithmetic was poor, and instead of being top, I came second. I was offered a vacancy at High School, but my parents were business people and they would have had to contribute to my fees. They considered a 'good' education wasted on a girl, so I remained at Whaddon, which I loved, anyway.

My ambition was to become a teacher 'like mother', but it was not to be. One of the sorrows of my early life was being unable to teach, but it helped my character no end! There were no solid foundations to my life, and I could have become an unbearable snob.

Soon after this, the upper school, to which our class graduated, adopted a most exciting form of education, devised by the Parents National Educational Union. There were many new and beautiful books; several extra subjects and a whole new form of procedure. Our form, the experimental one, was called Form 3. In this venture one's progress depended upon oneself. There was a lesson chart for the term and this was stuck on the wall. Responsibility for looking up the lesson rested on the pupils. We selected the necessary book and got on with it. Only if a pupil could not understand was the teacher's advice sought, otherwise the chapter was read until it was memorised and understood; the book was then put away and we wrote what we had learned. Our books were as difficult as any we would be expected to cope with, yet in this method of trust, most people made great advances. Only the slow ones needed the teacher, who had more time to give them.

Admittedly the procedure was easier for those accustomed to read for themselves than for children who needed to be told what to do, but it gave the teachers time to look after the weak ones and did not hold back those who were able to get ahead faster. Most were able to cope well.

Apart from our separate learning, there was a Shakespeare play to be learned thoroughly—a part committed to memory—and acted out each term. We were able to see this play acted by professionals at Gloucester Hippodrome, where repertory plays were performed most weeks. We read poetry both alone and as a class. During the summer the forms taking P.N.E.U. went out into the garden with the Head for poetry readings. Special happiness came from Longfellow's *Hiawatha*. Over and over again we read it in turn:-

'On the shores of Gitchi Gumee,
By the shining Big-Sea water,
Stood Nokomis, the old woman,
Pointing with her finger westward,
O'er the water pointing westward,
To the purple clouds of sunset.'

The garden under the big pear tree was forgotten; we were in the forest of Redwoods, looking where the old woman pointed, over the water into the sunset. It was magic!

The magic never worked so well indoors, and in the classroom readings sometimes became hilarious. There were the usual few who delighted themselves (and secretly all of us) by altering words here and there. There was one boy, Clarence Dowdeswell, whose name had always been altered to Ajie Dowdeswell. It was a simple matter to substitute 'Ajie Dowdeswell' for 'Ajie Dormo' and 'Ajie Dowdeswell—little squirrel' delighted the class and drove the master in charge mad. It all seems silly now, but one day we so maddened him that he threw a box of pencils at us in his fury. He had an urgent appointment with the Head after school and did not return the following term. We had one 'heavy' book each term, something to get our teeth into.

On the whole pupils enjoyed P.N.E.U. It is a system which enables those who wish to learn for themselves to do so. When I need or want to learn more, it is perfectly natural to go to the library, take out a book and read until the subject is mastered.

Mr Herrin spent many years at Whaddon School as its headmaster, remaining there—although he had better schools offered him—until his retirement. He gave the school the benefit of a lifetime's work and care and knew his pupils as he had known many of their parents. To his pupils he was always 'Boss Herrin'. To teachers and friends he was B.J.H. He disciplined the children in his care in a special way. He always referred to the girls as 'my girls'.

Thus, when one day I was caught stealing chalk (which was a craze just then), I was made to stand out in front of the class, while he told us all that he did not expect to find 'his girls' stealing chalk or anything else; he was ashamed of me and any others who had done this. I never stole chalk or anything else again, and have always retained a distaste for taking paper, pens or any other of the small things which so many of us pilfer as a matter of course today. If only there had been more Mr Herrins!

He put a stop to fighting in the girls' playground in the same way. He said, 'I expect boys to fight from time to time, but that my girls should do this is unthinkable'. He had a way of saying something, quite quietly, which shamed us, so that we remembered it and never repeated that particular misdemeanour. Perhaps it was because we knew he was our friend and would go to any lengths for his children, that we held Boss Herrin in such high regard.

Our schoolmaster and the village policeman were always in close collusion, and he knew of anything wrong committed on the way to or from school almost as soon as it happened. He considered that pupils were in his charge from the time they left their parents' care on their way to school until they once more arrived home after leaving school. When the policeman was seen crossing one of the school playgrounds, we knew that trouble was not far away. One instance of this was over an old lady who passed the school on her way to Gloucester from time to time. She was mentally ill and, although she was financially able to support herself, she was unable to dress properly. Sometimes her coat and skirt were shabby and tattered while her stockings and shoes were good; sometimes it was the other way round. She had a beard. She also always carried an umbrella. Everyone thought it was very funny to chant after her, 'Nanny, Nanny'. She would lay about her with her umbrella, and we had great fun dodging her. We were always quicker than she was.

The policeman, Mr Powell, our friend and protector, considered this behaviour on our part quite unacceptable and told Mr Herrin as much. This time the whole school was called from lessons into the hall and a stern lecture followed about the unkindness of treating someone who was obviously ill so badly. Such was his influence that no one called after her again.

On one occasion when Ben Herrin had been to France, attending a conference of headmasters, he returned with a motto for the school. This motto was printed in beautiful lettering all round the hall clock. It ran, 'Plus est en vous' and from that time onward he certainly believed that his pupils did have 'more in you' and he never let us forget it. He achieved a very high standard for his school.

He had a method even in those days which many teachers associate only with recent teaching practice; he discussed with us something we already knew about and went from there to something unfamiliar which he left us to explore. Thus when he and his family took out a mortgage on a new house, which was in itself an unusual thing for ordinary people to do in the 1920s, he called the house 'Long Leasowes', and asked us to find out what that meant. We all thought the answer was that it would be twenty years before the lease was paid and it was only comparatively recently that I was enchanted to discover that leasowe is an Old English word for meadow. His house had been built in a long meadow. He did not correct us, just said, 'Is that what you think?'

Mother was often ill at this time and it fell to my lot to look after the family. As I was beyond school-leaving age, my frequent absences were passed over, but having to be away from school made me very unhappy. The Head wanted me to stay on and take School Certificate with a view to entering teacher training college, but my parents thought otherwise and as, in turn, my sister and I left school, we were sent to the Gloucestershire College of Domestic Science for a short period each, 'because', mother said, 'you will need housecraft and cooking more than anything else'. The course was very useful; two places at the College were allocated to Country Schools at half-yearly intervals. Information from the Principal of the Gloucestershire College of Education says that the College records state, '1893: A scheme providing six months free training and maintenance for children from Gloucestershire Elementary Schools was developed this year'. We were referred to as 'the scholars', and the main purpose of the course was to prepare those concerned for work in domestic service. My passing out Certificate stated that I was now qualified as a kitchen maid, a post which I never took for payment, though early training was the impetus which persuaded me to learn as much as possible about housecraft, and practising it has never been difficult. After nearly a century of active life, the College is now closed.

On leaving the College, I went to a Gloucester family to begin learning to become a children's nurse. Service felt like being in prison after the freedom of childhood; being shut in a large garden for most of the day, amusing a small child was not what I wanted, but in those days there was no question of girls doing as they wanted; as a rule their parents decided for them.

I never really made a success of early adulthood. After leaving the job of children's nurse, I became apprenticed to a firm of bakers, working in the shop, but neither the proprietor nor I really thought that this was successful. My brother was now nearing sixteen and was due to leave his school in Gloucester. Of course, father wanted him to work in the business, hoping he would carry it on after his own retirement. My brother had his own ideas; his love lay in other directions, so it was decided that I should come home and continue to do the job I had known since childhood.

After leaving school, I met Mr Herrin for short talks on several occasions; the first was while I was waiting for father in Gloucester one day. About to pass me, he stopped his car and, leaning out of the window, asked, 'Why aren't you married yet?' My reply that I supposed I was waiting for the right man seemed to infuriate him. 'What do you want', he demanded, 'a millionaire?' and drove off too rapidly for a reply.

Money and a millionaire was not the object. Money — enough money to live on — is necessary, of course, but there is a much greater need than money. There must be affinity; people who take each other 'for better or worse' need to complement each other. Eventually 'my other half' came along, and we have been fortunate enough to enjoy many years of great happiness.

B.J.H. and I next met during the 1939 war. One afternoon, people working in the fields, in gardens, on the roads and in their homes, were suddenly made aware that some tremendous machine was bearing down on our village, then thundering down, and as people turned to face the approaching menace, between the trees a giant form was glimpsed, half filling the sky: a dark gigantic shape from which flames added their quota to the terror of the noise.

The burnt out plane lies as a twisted wreck in the field called Roundham, opposite the family house.

For perhaps half a minute folk watched as it dived lower, and lower, the wind screaming past its bulk. Then with a final crash like thunder, the thing hit soft earth in a field only a hundred yards from some houses. For a moment there was no sound except the crackling of flames.

As abruptly as the noise had ceased, the roar of the fire and the sound of an occasional explosion filled the air. Most people near by ran in the direction in which the plane — a medium bomber — had crashed. I was a quarter of a mile distant, but like everyone else felt drawn to the holocaust as if by a magnet. I had joined the Red Cross, and here might be an opportunity to put learning into practice. As we reached the field and surveyed the scene, we felt helpless. Some of the village people, including my father and mother, were already beside the tail of the plane, smashing a hole in it. The rear gunner was trapped there. In desperation he had kicked a small hole in the side of the plane. This was torn and chopped until it was large enough to reach inside, untangle him from the mass of wires surrounding him and pull him through.

One airman lay awkwardly on the grass. A young A.R.P. warden, who was also one of Colonel Sinnott's maids, Alice King, although normally very timid, had pulled him clear of the burning wreckage. We had no stretcher. Running back to the stile at the roadside, I was met by Diana Sinnott, to whom I quickly explained that we needed poles and a blanket. She ran back to the Grange for broomsticks and a blanket. We made a stretcher from these and carefully lifted the airman on to it. The men were pulling someone out through their jagged hole. The plane was an inferno and explosion sent debris and sparks higher even than the flames. We lost no time taking our airman away in one direction, as the men ran off with their charge in the other. One man was left — the pilot — but we knew there was no hope for him. The plane's nose was buried deep in the earth and fire enveloped the whole red-hot carcase of it. Police, firemen and ambulance arrived and no one was allowed near the raging fire, from the centre of which explosions still shook the earth from time to time. We had just finished splinting the airman's leg and the Ambulance men took over. We were free to look about us. There close beside us was B.J.H., quietly observing. He did not speak, and I hoped that perhaps I had justified his faith a little. The hospital complimented us on saving a badly broken leg from being shortened and the Air Ministry sent us their thanks. We learned that the pilot had been killed.

The men's hands were cut and bleeding, and none who had been on the scene slept that night.

At the end of the war, town sports were held in Gloucester, and our old friend was there. We walked to his house and he wondered sadly why, having so much potential, I had not been more successful. Sorrow for him filled my mind. He said he felt sure I could teach yet. I proved him right one day, but it was many years later, after his death. A great deal of character building was necessary first. One should be as complete a person as possible before trying to teach others and I was very incomplete. Humility, stability and many other of life's lessons had to be learned first.

Mr Herrin came to our wedding. It would not have been complete without him. When we had our first home, one large room and a small kitchen, he came to dinner one evening. He had retired and wished to become a member of the City Council. Seeing how frail he looked, we tried to dissuade him, but his mind was made up. He said he felt he had so much to give. Bless him, he always was a giver. He failed to gain a seat, and a few months later we heard that he had died.

As I was reading an account of Wordsworth's life and works recently, the following words from a series of sonnets, 'The River Duddon', took my attention:

-------------- be it so!
Enough, if something from our hands have power
To live, and act, and serve the future hour,
And if, as toward the silent tomb we go
Through love, through hope, and faith's transcendent dower
We feel that we are greater than we know.

He certainly lived through love, through hope and faith's transcendent dower. Did he ever feel that he was greater than he knew?

Chapter Nine   Hewers of Wood and Drawers of Water

Deut.xxix, 11

No one knows everybody in his village and we can only describe those we did know as we saw them. I ask forgiveness, therefore, for any omissions and for descriptions which may appear biased. In a village, people are individuals and are not typed according to their surroundings, as they may be when living in a block of flats or in houses in a particular street.

Several hundred years ago, Colonel Richard Atkyns of Tuffley, following the dictates of his conscience, rode with his men to try to save his King, Charles I. In the early half of this century our village had another Colonel who also, twice, took up arms for his King and country; a worthy successor to Colonel Atkyns and an example of what a village leader should be.

Edward Stockley Sinnott was born at Bedminster Down, Bristol on August 28th, 1868, and died at the home of his daughter and son-in-law, Colonel and Mrs Hugh Tyler of Beacon Cottage, Trellech, Monmouth, on August 8th, 1969. His life was a full one, generously given. To him and his family, living at the Grange meant caring for the village and its people. Theirs was a way of life which has disappeared.

The squire of the village (or his equivalent) might appear to an outsider to be the possessor of a great many advantages and privileges; he often had a large and beautiful house with extensive grounds, and enjoyed a gracious life-style. But, if he took his position seriously, his responsibilities were enormous. During the early part of this century, when travel was difficult and slow, the Grange always kept a well-stocked medicine chest, ready to treat any emergency, and, as the family possessed a telephone many years before anyone else in the village, it was made clear to us that we could go there for help at any time of the day or night. An instance of what a boon this was occurred during the 1939 war.

A crippled bomber aeroplane had crash-landed in fields at the far end of the village from us at two o'clock one morning. One of the airmen, a French Canadian, who spoke very little English, came to our door and begged to be let in. He had been to most of the houses in the village, but people were afraid he was an enemy. We took him in and learned the details of the incident, and then went straight to the Grange. The Colonel immediately organised the necessary help and turned out the Home Guard, with the result that the crew were all found and taken to safety, and information sent to the Air Base concerned.

Colonel Sinnott learned to use a rifle while at school at Clifton College and was a member of two winning Ashburton Shield teams. He trained as a civil engineer and continued competitive shooting. He held a commission in the South Midland Royal Engineers (Territorials) and volunteered for service in the South African War in 1900.

On his return home, he was engaged in railway and dock development in the Port Talbot, Glamorgan area, where he met his future wife. They were married in 1905. For a while the family lived at Llandaff, where two sons, James and Edward were born. They moved to Tuffley Grange in 1907 and the Colonel took up the appointment as County Surveyor for Gloucestershire on the 1st January, 1908. He continued with his Territorial connection, bicycling to the range at Matson for shooting practice, and attended annual camps.

At the outbreak of the 1914 war, he joined up and went to France, where he assisted in organising the maintenance of lines of communication, roads and bridges, to keep men and supplies moving. He was mentioned in despatches and in 1916 was appointed Commander of the Order of St. Michael and St. George (C.M.G.). In 1919 he was made Deputy Lieutenant for the County of Gloucestershire.

Five daughters were born to the Sinnotts at Tuffley Grange: Carew, Elinor, Sylvia, Vivien and Diana.

On taking up his work again as County Surveyor after the War, the Colonel

Colonel E. S. Sinnott.

found the roads of the County all in need of repair and maintenance. No work had been carried out on them while the war was in progress, so he set about rectifying the run-down conditions.

His life was marked by many tragedies, the first of which was the death of his son Edward in 1916. His wife died in 1920, when their youngest daughter was thirteen months old. There are big memorial windows to both of them in St. Margaret's Church, Whaddon.

The Colonel remarried in 1922. His second wife, a nurse, worked hard to secure a District Nurse for our village, as she was appalled to find that a village, as isolated as ours was from the nearest town, was without medical aid. She succeeded in having a bungalow specially built for her at Whaddon, so that help was always at hand.

The second Mrs Sinnott was enlightened beyond her time and recognised the importance of the Women's Institute as a means of spreading education. She was an ardent member of the movement, bringing matters that she felt needed urgent attention before the Committee, persuading those who hitherto had accepted their lot as inevitable to try to build a better environment. A firm believer in democracy, she stirred sluggish souls to vote and vote again. Tuffley awoke from the lethargy of ages and became a village aware that progress could be achieved by listening and then petitioning.

She was a most careful manager of her own household and saw to it that anyone under her roof who needed help of any kind got it. Thus when one of her maids was found to be walking with difficulty, she was taken to London for examination and special shoes were made for her. The Sinnott children were encouraged to go barefoot whenever possible so that their feet grew strong. Mrs Sinnott continued her crusade for progress in our village for many years until a sad and very trying illness put a stop to it. She died in 1943.

Colonel Sinnott was meticulous in the care he gave to his land, making it as productive as possible; his orchards and colonies of bees, mentioned elsewhere in these pages, were typical examples of his industry.

He took a great interest in St. Margaret's Church, and his family were always available to give assistance when it was needed. The restoration and enlargement of the churchyard was the Colonel's main interest, and a care and maintenance scheme was set up which ran very successfully, his chief assistant being Miss Dorothy Thomas.

He also served on the Diocesan Board of Finance and, on his retirement from the office of Surveyor in 1936, he became treasurer and prime mover behind the Friends of Gloucester Cathedral, an association which had been inaugurated the previous year. He was successful in increasing the membership until its numbers were second only to those of Canterbury. During his regime, all legacies had to be invested and the resulting income remains of great benefit to the Friends of the Cathedral. Mrs Anne Butt was the Colonel's 'right hand man' at the Cathedral and she has been honoured by having the sixth bell in the tower named after her — 'Nan's Bell'.

World War II brought further grief to the Grange, when the family learned that James, who was married and had two daughters, had been killed at Halfaya Pass in 1941. He was serving as Major with the Royal Gloucestershire Hussars. His children were doubly orphaned when their mother was later killed in an accident, but their uncle and aunt, Colonel and Mrs Tyler, took care of them until they were grown up.

Soon after the Colonel's second wife died in 1943, his father came to end his

The Grange.

days at the Grange. He was almost 100 years old when he died.

After his father's death, Colonel Sinnott left the Grange. All his family were settled elsewhere and he went to live with his brother at Clifton. While staying there he paid frequent visits to Colonel and Mrs Tyler and, eventually, went to live with them permanently in 1968, dying when he was just twelve days short of his 101st birthday! Our village was fortunate in having such a distinguished family at the Grange for so long.

Although he was so accomplished, the Colonel was a very human person. He took all his duties seriously and the many tragedies in his life made him very kind and compassionate to others in distress. He shared our sorrows and worries and we, in turn, grieved with him in his sadness. Once he showed me the beautiful full-length portrait of his first wife and later, when his son James died, he asked me into the house one day, saying 'he wanted me to see something'. There, hanging in the light from a large window was another large portrait. He took me across to it and showed it with great pride and sadness. The picture was of his son, James, in full uniform. To me it looked magnificent and I was deeply touched and affected at the thought that he should want to share it with me in this way.

Mrs Sylvia Bell, the third daughter of the family, told me how her father used to say to her, 'Some people are destined to be hewers of wood and drawers of water'. What more could anyone wish to be? Those who draw water for others provide the most essential element of life. Without water nothing can live; while wood supplies the fires to warm and comfort people, to cook food and create power.

The respect accorded this exceptional family was natural then, though we were quite unaware that some of the Colonel's daughters chafed at the privileges which gave them more than the rest of us. They disliked the idea of village people having to use the side door instead of the front one, when they came up to the Grange. They avoided going through the village when they had cars before we did, even though their cars were small ones. To us this was life as it was lived then; to them the conditions needed changing. Throughout their lives they have used their abilities to bring about advancement for others. Like their parents before them, all the Sinnott daughters made their individual contribution to the community in which they lived.

Our village had no shop until some time in the 1920s. One of the rooms in our house had been built and fitted out as a shop before we came to live at Grange Villa, but as previously mentioned, our house was situated at the end of a row of houses, and a shop needs to be central to be successful, so that our family never made use of it for that purpose. Families used to manage from one week to the next with what food they had in the house and garden, going to the city perhaps once a week, returning with laden shopping bags full of those things which could not be grown at home nor bartered for from a neighbour. Swopping was rife!

The children never felt the need for a shop until one actually appeared. There were precious few outings and not many sweets. The icecream van came round each week and we could buy a loaded cornet for a penny or a 'wafer' for twopence. There was also a fish and chip van, on which the fish and chips were cooked as it went along. Both vans were always surrounded as soon as they stopped. I've never tasted such delicious chips! The smell was wonderful.

In our house, my father, who went into Gloucester daily, did most of the shopping. Mother just gave him a list of the things she wanted. He used to bring us sweets every week, generally alternating between a slab of chocolate and a cake of Edinburgh rock. Sometimes there was home-made toffee. The last two were made by a Scottish lady, who sold them in her shop in the City. They were very good and nourishing, but there was no variety and we could not buy them ourselves. Many children, like us, were too young to walk to the Post Office at Upper Tuffley, where there was always a wonderful selection. At one time, dad tried making toffee himself, but our range fire was fierce, and the toffee was liable to boil over and get burnt. Burnt toffee tasted dreadful!

It was a red-letter day for the village when an American lady—a widow, I believe—came and opened a shop—one just for children. The shop could not be seen from the front of her house; the contents, sweets and tops, were kept on a wide shelf inside a window, on which we knocked to get attention. The shelf was raised at the back and came right up to the window, so we could have a good look before deciding on what we wanted.

Mrs Pearson, the owner, was middle-aged and plump, with a soft, attractive American accent. She always wore a shiny, high-necked black blouse and over her large, comfortable bosom were draped several rows of chains and beads. Among the chains and necklaces was a black ribbon, from which dangled a pair of *pince-nez* spectacles. Before opening the window, she adjusted these on her nose so that she could see us better, then she surveyed her prospective customers expectantly. She made several kinds of sweets herself, as well as stocking manufactured ones, and her speciality was toffee apples. These were apples, stuck on sticks and thickly coated with crunchy toffee. As soon as one child saw that she had them, the news fled round the village and everyone knew about it. As a rule the toffee apples were delicious, but occasionally the apples were sour, and biting through the sugary crust into a sour apple was agonising.

Mrs Pearson was deeply interested in children and talked to us about our own lives, but when we asked her about herself, she became sad and said that she missed 'Amurrica' very much and wanted to go back there. She was always saying, 'I'm going back to Amurrica' and one day she did, in fact, return and for a time we were without a shop. We missed Mrs Pearson very much.

Then a real general shop opened in the centre of Grange Road, run by a family named Bailey, in their front room. Children were not allowed inside unless they had grocery lists, but were still expected to knock on the window to get attention if they wanted to buy sweets. This was because the shop was small and children take a lot of time and space when choosing sweets, so we had all the time we wanted and all the space the front path afforded while we made our choice.

This shop lasted for some years and then was handed over to Miss Wixey, who had a large detached house a little further along the road.

Miss Wixey kept cats. She took in every stray cat which came her way and though we very rarely saw them, we heard them mewing in the back of the house. She told us the history of each one of them and sometimes actually showed us one. She had over a dozen at one time and must have needed the shop to pay for all their food. Miss Wixey's shop continued to flourish for many years. As we grew older, we used to walk as far as the Stroud road and when we had finished our work in the mornings, we patronised Mrs Pritchard at the Post

Office. Her shop was stocked with a great deal of food and sweets of every variety. Poor Mrs Pritchard used to get very bothered over our picking and choosing. Shopkeepers, then, made very little profit from their sweets; each halfpennyworth had to tip the scale. Mrs Pritchard got so used to knowing just how many sweets were required to do this, that she would count them out.

Very few things were wrapped or packeted. Sugar was done up in strong blue sugar paper, which can still be bought at stationers for use as drawing paper. Mr Herrin, during one of his general knowledge sessions, was once discussing the future. In an age when we travelled by bike and vegetables and nearly everything else had to be wrapped up after being purchased, or were simply put into our shopping bags as they were, he said, 'One day you will not be able to buy unwrapped goods. All vegetables will be washed and trimmed and everything will be prepackaged'. He told us that most workpeople in America went to work in cars, and we could not envisage a time when these things would all apply to us. I remember thinking about items of food, 'but they would be bound to be more expensive'. That wasn't wrong either! Our sweets were going to be tipped from the scales into cornet shaped bags, and very sticky they became after being clutched in hot hands for a while! The shopkeepers worked much harder then and also put up with many things from their customers that they would not tolerate in these days.

Shops were places where people met and discussed the local news. Very few had time to attend 'coffee mornings', so places where we met while still going about our work were very welcome.

Haymaking brought together everyone in the vicinity who could possibly spare the time. It was a sort of working holiday, plenty of hard work, lots of fun and laughter. That kind of haymaking disappeared with the coming of the combine. One man can drive the machine, which cuts and later on bales the hay. The fun has gone.

Early in the 1920s, our hay was still cut by a man wielding a scythe, as he patiently and steadily worked his way round the field. Large fields needed several men, who worked one behind the next, each cutting a swathe. Even when horse-drawn mowers and then motor mowing machines came, it was still useful to have a swathe scythe-cut round the outside of the field, and in an orchard, unless the trees are very widely separated, scything is still the only safe way of cutting long grass.

When the grass was cut and considered dry enough to rake, all the men and women who could spare the time came along to help, raking the hay into small 'wallies' (as we called them), and then incorporating three small rows into one large one, and finally making haycocks, large heaps, convenient for the waggon to take. To make hay while the sun shone was everyone's dream, but in our variable climate, it often rained. Hay must be dry when it is ricked, otherwise heat builds up inside and the stack goes on fire. Sometimes, when the weather had been wet for a long time, the new grass grew up through the cut hay, making the work still harder. Once I raked over a wasp's nest, which had been made after the hay had been cut; I got stung all over. In the country, however, that was considered all part of the day's work.

The children came into the hayfields after school, when their mothers brought the tea. There was always lemonade in a huge jug and a gallon jar of cider under the waggon. Mother would make tea in an enamel pot, which held a gallon, and bring a basket of bread and butter and cheese and salad with her. Between tea and a late bedtime, we had hayfights or worked with the grown-ups when there were forks or rakes to spare. Sitting round the waggon was the time for talk—children listened in those days unless they were addressed and we learned a lot.

The most exciting thing about haymaking or any harvesting was riding home to the farm on top of the swaying load of hay or corn. Harvest time was always, or nearly always, fun, and with all the hard work we had a great deal of happiness, but that last load home was a triumph. Harvest Home really meant something in those days, it was a live and wonderful time.

Old Bill became known to us through haymaking. He and his wife came to live in Grange Road when they were between 50 and 60 years old. Their real names were 'Mr and Mrs William Moss', but Old Bill was never anything else to the adults, though we children had to address him properly.

Bill was one of the casualties of high unemployment between the wars and for years he was unable to get a job, so he often came and helped us. He loved haymaking.

Bill was short and rotund. He wore a scarlet and white spotted neckerchief during the week. Most of the men had one of these and they were put to many uses. Very often they were filled with bread and cheese and an onion to eat at midday and when, after the meal, the sun was at its hottest, they were knotted at each corner and used as a sunhat. Bill was a good worker and he always had a fund of stories. One particular tale he told us every year and while we sat in the shade of the waggon eating our tea, we waited for it.

The tale was about a girl—a Londoner, Bill said. He always began: 'I knew a gal, a Londoner 'er was, married so and so, and 'er used to say 'er didn' know what a rake was. Well, one day 'er was runnin' over the wallies an' a rake covered wi' hay were under one of 'em. Well, 'er trod on the teeth o' this yer rake, an' the 'andle come up an' 'it 'er smartly on the nose. 'Er told us more names for that there rake than we ever knowed!' Bill told this story so well, that we never tired of hearing it, and it always brought a laugh.

He was a very good gardener, and with his pig and some hens, he made the family pretty well self-sufficient. He was a good grower of flowers, too, and one of the few people to lay down lawns at the front of his house. Most flowers in the village were grown from slips, divided roots, or seeds handed from one villager to another; so we all had the basic old-fashioned ones, such as primroses, and polyanthus, pinks, carnations, wallflowers, Sweet Williams, antirrhinums, roses, peonies, etc., and in the good soil, they thrived. In addition, every gardener tried to grow one speciality. The speciality, however, remained distinctive only until its owner started giving bits or seeds to his neighbour. Bill's speciality was a huge syringa tree, which he had trained all over the front of his house. Its blossoms were exceptionally large and the scent in the stillness of a summer evening or early morning was almost overpowering. The sprays of flowers covered the branches, and were filled with bees on fine days. Soon syringa bushes with extra large flowers and a beautiful scent were growing all over the village.

Like the rest of us, Bill rode a bicycle to Gloucester. He maintained a slow, stately pace, which nothing would make him alter. He cheerfully let anyone pass him, bidding them 'Good morning' or 'Good evening' as the case might be. One day, on her way home to lunch, my sister thought she would hurry him up. She rode up alongside him and they talked a little, then Naomi said, 'Come on, Mr Moss, we'll have to hurry or I'll be late getting back to work'. Bill did not change his pace a little bit, and answered steadily, 'Look 'ere, young Name, I wasn't built in a hurry. I've got two speeds, slow and stop!' No one would alter him. 'Young Name' rode on ahead.

During times of drought, Bill cleaned and repaired the wells which dried up and he used to tell us how once he found bindweed at the bottom of a 20 foot well; the roots were still growing down.

Bill and my father both made home-made wine, and they would sit and talk for hours over a couple of glasses. The men used to visit those people who had the same interests as themselves, and one evening Dad and Bill arranged to go to Minchinhampton on the motorbike and sidecar to see Bill's sister. Bill said she grew the largest cauliflowers her had ever seen. She also brewed home-made wine. They went early one spring evening to see those cauliflowers and during the course of the evening, several glasses of home-made wine were drunk.

It was pitch dark as they began their return journey across the Common. Cows and horses are always a hazard there; the grazing is free to certain people during the summer months and the animals stray all over the roads, most of which are unlit. When they were well out on to the Common, suddenly, without warning, the bike hit a large object and climbed over it. They stopped a few yards further on and went back, fearing the worst. The animal which they had hit was a horse, which had been lying asleep across the road. As they reached it, to their relief the horse got up, rather stiffly, and slowly ambled off across the Common. It appeared to be none the worse for its adventure. They took extra care on the rest of the homeward journey.

Bill had an unusual grace which he always said after meals. It ran:

Some was hard and some was tough
But, thank the Lord, I've had enough.

We knew him well enough to take it with equanimity.

Our old friend frequently suffered from bronchitis during the winter months and I last saw him when I visited Mr and Mrs Moss with mother one bitterly cold winter night. He was breathing very heavily and his wife said that the Doctor did not expect him to live very much longer. He died during the night and his small, frail wife was left alone to tend the house and the large garden. We thought about his grace and how suitable it would have been as his epitaph.

Post ladies delivered the mail in our straggling village lanes as far back as any of us could remember. Mrs Mortimer did it until she became too old and, then, Mrs Meredith took over. When her time came to retire, other ladies carried on the service in turn. They came round twice daily and collected mail left in the pillar-box after doing the deliveries. As the pillar-box was opposite our house, posting letters was easy. I've never been so lucky since I left Tuffley. They each wore a navy uniform and hat and looked very smart with black shoes and stockings. Their bicycles were fitted with the same kind of frame at the front to carry the heavy mail bag as is used today. In bad weather they were often wet through when they reached us, and there was still a long way to go between us and Tuffley Farm. The Toots were two houses which could only be reached by crossing fields, but the ladies never made any complaints. They tried to reach the end of their round in the morning by 8.30, so that people had their letters as early as possible. We were well served by the Post Ladies.

Mrs Hayward was a very special character in Lower Tuffley. Long before the village had a District Nurse, Mrs Hayward was the midwife who delivered most of our babies. She had probably done the same for their parents. It was nothing unusual to see her coming down a path from the house to the road at 6.30am smiling happily. She would give anyone interested enough to listen full details of the baby's sex and weight and how long it had taken to arrive, but she never, as far as I knew, divulged anything of the family's business. She would be laden with sheets for washing and within a couple of hours they would be billowing, shining white, on her clothes-line. She would continue to look after the mother, and sleep seemed a quite unnecessary thing to her when she was thus engaged. She was always happy and cheerful and businesslike.

Mrs Hayward was a tiny person, like a bright bird. She had, unfortunately, a cleft palate, an affliction which, in those days, rendered the sufferer almost incapable of making himself or herself understood. This had no effect on Mrs Hayward, however, we understood her perfectly; she left no one in any doubt as to what she meant. Coping with birth and death was bread and butter to her. In another society she would have been the village Head Woman. If anything unusual happened, she always let us know about it and told everyone what he or she was expected to do! If anyone was getting married or leaving the village, Mrs Hayward appeared on the doorstep, notebook and pencil in hand, and her coat had deep pockets! We would be informed who was doing what and she would say: 'We're collecting for a present'. Everybody contributed. Likewise, when someone died, we would hear her knock. She would say: 'You've heard about Mr So-and-so, haven't you? Well, we're collecting for a wreath'. We added to the collection.

Was there a whist drive or concert at any of the local halls, Mrs Hayward sold all the tickets, naturally, and usually the room would be full. She was indefatigable.

When the Church Fete was imminent, she and a companion would arrive carrying a huge clothes basket between them. 'We're collecting for the fete', she'd say. We gave. She continued her labours until she was a great age. No one really knew how old she was until she died.

Before Lower Tuffley had cars or a bus, Mrs Hayward found out about charabancs. They were the forerunners of the modern coach and the earliest ones had solid tyres. There was no fixed top to the vehicle, only a huge hood, which had to be manhandled right over the body when it rained.

A charabanc held about 25 to 30 people; the seats went right across from one side to the other, with a door to each row. Once Mrs Hayward had found out about these handy vehicles, the village had a wonderful time. She and the driver would decide on a venue and then she would come round collecting so much a head until the trip was paid for. These trips were called 'Outings'. Early on the Day, everyone who was going assembled at a given point to await the arrival of the charabanc and when it arrived all filed in. Great skill was required in arranging the seating, because we had our feuds like every other village and, generally, there would be one family who was not speaking to another. They had to be widely separated. Likewise, there were always bosom pals, usually numbering more than one seat would hold, who insisted that they must all sit together. Mrs Hayward coped. After her death, the Outings were carried on by Mrs Haines and Ernie, but they let themselves be worried by people's vagaries, whereas Mrs Hayward had just given an awkward customer a piece of her mind, if necessary!

Our next-door neighbours, the Merrimans, were memorable more for the things which happened through them, rather than for themselves. Mrs Merriman made very good bread and, if we were ill, she always came round with a newly-baked loaf for us, all hot from the oven. Illness could be enjoyable.

Their neighbours remembered them chiefly on account of a magpie they kept in a cage, letting it out for exercise from time to time. He was a beautiful bird, his white feathers were always gleaming and the black parts shone with a green lustre. He had black, beady eyes. What else could he be called but Jacko? Like all magpies, he loved bright, colourful things and my mother always put hair ribbons on my sister and me; they were blue, pink or red. As we ran up our steps into the yard, Jacko would hear us and fly up on a roof from which he had a splendid view of prospective plunder. He always seemed to know, too, when either of us was in the closet and would come and stand in the square ventilation hole, waiting for us to emerge.

When he spied a hair ribbon, his day was made. He descended on to the head of his victim and divested her of her ribbon, quickly and neatly. Until we were rescued, our screams rivalled the bird's raucous squawks. The hair ribbon was carried off in triumph by Jacko and was retrieved only when Mrs Merriman was able to extract it from his hideaway while he was absent.

The Merrimans' sons, together with some of their friends, ran a mandolin and banjo band, and formed a kind of pierrot concert party. They practised in a room just below our bedroom and my sister and I always knew their songs and pieces by heart before the time of the concert came. We were supposed to be asleep, but we vastly enjoyed that concert party.

Our village had its share of invalids, but being unwell was no excuse for being inactive in those days. This was demonstrated by several families, who found employment for themselves, even though they were incapacitated in some way or another.

The Money family, who lived at Wyndyates on the Stroud road, were a fine example of this spirit of independence. Mrs Money and one son were the only ones out of a family of six who were well. All the children had had polio and were badly handicapped. Mr Money limped heavily, Kenneth needed two sticks to get about, and so it went on. Kenneth earned his living repairing watches and clocks; the two girls had a loom and wove beautiful material and sold it, as well as making many craft articles; Irene painted; Mr and Mrs Money managed, cleaned and ran the two Y.M.C.A. huts. They kept them spotlessly clean, provided meals, and saw to bookings and arrangements. At Christmas time there were always two huge parties for the children, one for those over and one for those under twelve years old. There were Christmas trees which reached to the ceiling and were decorated all over and hung with gifts — one good game or toy for each child. These were provided by the Y.M.C.A. The Money family also kept a missionary Coffee House (they were Quakers); this, too, was spotless and I remember going to a meeting of the Brownies there. They also ran a Sunday School, which was well attended. They all died fairly young, the last to go being Kenneth, who had been left alone for some time.

Ida Thomas lived at Fox Elms in Upper Tuffley. She was confined to a wheel chair with spinal trouble. This did not prevent her from running the St. Barnabas Guide company for many years. She made the hours spent in her wheel chair an opportunity for learning more about Guiding and as Captain, she ran one of the best companies around. It was a common sight to see her, surrounded by laughing, chattering Guides, being pushed to or from some visit. She took her company and they took her, to camp regularly for many years. She died relatively young, but her life was an inspiration to any of us who felt hard done by.

Jeff Moss was a tragic case of tuberculosis. He and his family lived at a small farm off Tuffley lane. They kept a few cows and, until he became too ill, Jeff delivered milk in two pails, suspended from a yoke. A measure hung inside one of the pails. When he became very ill, Donald Hall, himself disabled, and a shoe repairer, organised the children to make collections of Woodbine packets to buy a wheel chair for Jeff. We needed many thousands, but the children spent their spare time going round the village houses, collecting the used Woodbine packets until we had gathered enough. Poor Jeff died before his chair was available.

Courage, self-help and responsibility for our neighbour were a way of life for us.

Chapter Ten   Parting Day

The heart of the hamlet of Lower Tuffley, together with the village of Whaddon, was, until the late 1930s, the church of St. Margaret. Upper Tuffley was cared for by the little St. Barnabas, now rebuilt in a beautiful, modern architectural style. In the 'thirties, a new local church, St. George's, was built in Grange Road. Until then most of the village babies were brought to St. Margaret's to be baptised in the ancient stone font; almost all our young men and girls were married there; and, until the late 1920s, when even after enlargement, it was too small, the churchyard was the final resting-place of those who died. Thomas Grey's *Elegy Written in a Country Churchyard* sums up the essence of this peaceful place, as it does for so many a country churchyard.

The church itself is lovely in its ancient simplicity. The main body dates from the thirtheenth century, the tower, added later, is five hundred years old, while the foundations are thought to have been there for a thousand years. It stands on a slight mound and the tower is visible from some distance away.

The alteration of the parish boundary severely handicapped the little church and its true parishioners are now few, but those who are left work hard to maintain their great heritage and endeavour to keep faith and continuity with the past.

The approach from the direction of Gloucester, through Lower Tuffley and Whaddon Green, was one of the most beautiful in the country. On each side of the Stroud road were massive elm trees, forming an avenue, their branches meeting overhead. Colonel Sinnott's daughter, Carew Tyler, maintains that they were planted to commemorate the Battle of Waterloo, so that it is not surprising that by the 1920s concern was felt lest they were becoming dangerous because of their great age. On the other hand, their beauty made it difficult to take the decision to fell them. I remember hearing the vicar and my father debating the point after a large bough had fallen across the Stroud road during a dry summer. Dad could not envisage any useful purpose in keeping them, while the vicar ruminated on what good coffins the timber would make. I felt very sad.

Colonel Sinnott could look beyond the immediate future. He tried to persuade Colonel Jeune (who then held the manor of Whaddon) to replant the avenue with young trees, before the old elms were felled. The scheme, however, was considered too costly and nothing was done. Now, many years must pass before the trees, chestnuts and oaks, which were eventually planted, reach maturity and form another gracious avenue, making an

Whaddon Green.

imposing approach to the church.

Most of the massive elms were felled in the early 1950s, after several limbs had fallen dangerously. Their final disgrace came when one tree dropped a heavy bough right across a seat which had been donated by William Bellows, a well-known Gloucester printer and publisher. Oaks and chestnuts were planted together, so that by the time the chestnuts were ready for felling, the oaks would be large enough to take over.

Elizabeth Vowles says that the work done by Colonel Sinnott, when churchwarden and general finance secretary, is still showing its worth. Although with many of the devoted friends of St. Margaret's whom he knew, he has gone to 'the bosom of his Father and his God', and although some of those still living are too old or too ill to continue the work of caring for this little church, it is thanks to those past labourers and to those who still carry the torch, that St. Margaret's remains, and stands as it stood in the thirteenth century when it was built. The winding churchyard path, sunk between grassy borders, still leads to the small porch and through the old oak door, into an atmosphere compounded of many elements — carols at Christmas, Easter joy, Harvest thanksgiving, centuries of prayer and praise, grief of many mourners, joy and happiness of a multitude of worshippers, all combined into an enveloping calm.

As we and our friends grew older, our lives were bound up with this small church, as were those of most of the village folk. It seemed the most permanent thing in a century when all about us was change. We grew up while village and church relationships were as they had been through hundreds of years. The two Colonels, Jeune and Sinnott, vicar's and people's warden respectively, several farming families, as well as ordinary parishioners like ourselves, loved St. Margaret's and found there a spiritual home.

Times of both grief and joy found release within its walls and were marked by gifts which lasted — oak choir stalls from a farmer and his wife, stained glass windows commemorating those, known to many of us, who had died, the sadness of whose passing was softened by this evidence of a family's love, memorial tablets to the dead of two world wars, all tell their stories for those who wish to learn. They are kept clean and shining by friends who keep faith through the years.

While the congregation was still a large one, it was not difficult to add the few simple necessities to keep the church flourishing, but smaller boundaries and the slaughter caused by the wars altered circumstances drastically. Some of the windows, the tablets, the eagle lectern, are memorials to people who would have been active participants in the life of the church, continuing the work of their fathers; whose death robbed small parishes of their male supporters, leaving the women to contend with all the necessary care involved in running and maintaining the country church. Many people found work — or husbands — away from home; villages were no longer a close community, evacuees and an influx of new residents broke the old harmony and time will be needed for readjustment.

During the late 'forties, the time came when St. Margaret's needed at least £1,000 to be spent on it, if it were not to become a ruin. The problem this presented was formidable, but the congregation drew up their plan of action. Through the Appeal Secretary, Dorothy Thomas, leaflets were distributed far beyond the parish boundary (one reached me in Surrey) and, although those responsible feared for the outcome of the project, they never wavered in their determination to do their utmost to carry it out. Everyone who had known and loved the church was alerted and contributions began to flow in. Compromises had to be made, but in the end most of the essential work, such as repairing roof timbers, retiling with Cotswold tiles, replacing guttering, redecoration and renovating, was complete. The little church still stands, calmly beautiful, a silent witness to the faith of countless generations.

In the past, the church also supplied many of the earthly needs of the poor, the widows and the elderly. Whaddon church used to give 5 cwts of coal to each needy person in Whaddon and Lower Tuffley, while oranges and calico were distributed at Brookthorpe through the charity of one of the church families. Lilian remembers helping to deliver the latter. Oranges were brought within poor people's reach, and the calico was used for making underclothing and bed linen.

The annual church fete, which was held in rotation at Brookthorpe Vicarage, Whaddon Manor or Tuffley Grange, was the social highlight of the year. The vicarage at Brookthorpe, the Manor at Whaddon and the Grange at Tuffley all had beautiful lawns, and wherever the fete was held, the gardens were open to all from the three parishes. The entire population came — as and when work allowed — to take part. Preparations went on for months beforehand (everyone was expected to contribute something for the stalls), tea was served on the lawns when fine or indoors if wet; plays were performed, or there was a display of country dancing or the children's dancing class; and there was always a diversity of competitions and bowling for a live pig. Some of the men went on competing for the pig until they had paid far more than it would have cost them to buy one. All this made a great deal of work for our elders, but resulted in a vast family party each year. One of the remembered delights was ice-cream (the real stuff from a freezing canister) in which whole strawberries had been mixed, until it was pink coloured and strawberry flavoured.

The fete always ended with a dance. When this was held at the Manor, it was a real barn dance, taking place in the tithe barn. The floor might be dusty and uneven, but the atmosphere! A 'three piece band'—piano, drums and either violin or saxophone—oil lamps hanging from the beams, children and young people dancing, the older ones sitting round talking, laughing and just enjoying it all. No one, except perhaps the country dancers, performed very well (though we all thought we did), there was never anything stronger than lemonade to drink, there were cakes and sandwiches to eat, and life was very happy. The service at church the next day was for a real family.

During the 1920s, the churchyard became almost full, and new land was given to enlarge it. Parishioners, including the Colonels and the Vicar, and members of the Church Council, set to and helped fence the land and level the ground; the only cost was for timber, nails and suchlike things. There was even a cuckoo gate, to keep cows out, while admitting would-be churchgoers.

St. Margaret's is rectangular in shape. Its pews were of oak, dark with age. At the back of the church there are some small ones which had, originally, been used by shepherds. There the men could sit with their dogs and, if the necessity arose, could go out without disturbing others of the congregation. When we were young, old coloured tiles covered the aisle. As we grew up, the church like the village progressed through three kinds of lighting. First, there were oil lamps, giving off a homely smell of warm paraffin; then came Aladdin lamps, which gave a brilliant light, but hissed continually and had to be

Some of the individuals responsible for building the timber fence at the enlarged churchyard. Left to right: the Rev. Thomas E. Johnson (vicar), Mr Johnson (verger), my father, Colonel Sinnott (people's warden) and Colonel Jeune (vicar's warden).

pumped up from time to time. Electricity superseded these in turn. Electricity also provided the power for blowing a beautiful reed organ, given by Mr Owen Lee-Williams, in memory of his father, Dr Charles Lee-Williams, who had been organist at Gloucester Cathedral and who cared for churches all round the city. His son often worshipped at Whaddon. Music is a strongly emphasised subject in Gloucester, with the cathedral providing concerts of organ, symphony and chamber music, as well as great choral works (the Three Choirs Festival visits Gloucester, Worcester and Hereford Cathedrals in turn).

Groups of schoolchildren used to visit the cathedral from time to time to be introduced to great organ music and musicians; thus we were fortunate enough to hear Edward Elgar, Herbert Brewer, Herbert Sumsion and Charles Lee-Williams playing and explaining some of their own works. A cathedral packed with children is a wonderful sight and those of us who were able to take part in these outings found that the experience spread a great love of music right through our generation. As members of the choir at Whaddon, we found music natural and rewarding, and when our organ was consecrated, we sang Dr Lee-Williams' lovely setting to the anthem 'Thou wilt keep him in perfect peace'.

Although methods of lighting changed, heating came from a well stoked Tortoise stove, which warmed the whole building to such an extent that after a bitterly cold walk to church on a winter evening, we all tended to grow sleepy—until the vicar spotted us. Our vicar had a very effective way of dealing with those who were not attending to the service. He stood quite quiet, glaring hard at the culprit; the cat-napper was hastily nudged awake by his neighbour, and the service proceeded.

We used to time our journey to church by the bells. The deep bell tolled for five minutes and then was silent for five. This was repeated by the tenor bell, but the last, the treble, rang for only a short time, and we knew that if we were not near when it began, we must run, or be late and run the gauntlet of outraged stares from those who had managed to be early.

There were many fascinating things to look at in church. Beautifully polished vases holding flowers; the shining cross and candlesticks; tall diamond-paned windows with pointed arches; memorials to previous worshippers; and a large hatchment bearing the arms of George III over the vestry door. While the Jeune family held the manor, the flowers were always grown there, and were arranged in the church by Mrs Jeune, simply but very beautifully. I have a particular recollection of red geraniums and large white daisies at Whitsuntide. They shone brightly against the old cream walls.

Only two bells remain now. The big, deep bell, which was used for funerals, we knew as 'the passing bell'. At the time of death, it was a means of communication. It tolled three times three if a man had died, and two times three for a woman. We of the village listened and counted. If we did not know at once 'for whom the bell tolled', we soon found out. When the bells needed recasting and rehanging after World War II, the passing bell was found to be cracked and, as it was not of great age, it was given for melting down as payment for the repair of the other two.

Many happy hours were spent by the children of Tuffley and Whaddon in and around the church. There was a good choir then—eight or so boys, the same number of girls, and three or four men. We met regularly each week, sometimes more than once, for choir practice. If we were early, or had time on our hands for some reason or other, the headstones of the graves were a constant source of interest. We cleaned them so that we could read the ancient inscriptions. One, which was considered very amusing, was dedicated to a long-dead lady called Eliza Long Knapp. Even the vicar thought 'Here lies Eliza Long Knapp' was funny. 'Well, she certainly is having one', he would say.

One particular grave was the responsibility of our family's youngsters to keep tidy and provided with fresh flowers. It was that of a young girl of 10, whom we had known since she was a baby. Her name was Muriel Treasure and she was the adopted daughter of an old lady who had already reared a large family of her own. She saw this baby orphan and in spite of the entreaties of her own daughters, who knew their mother was too old to be able to look after Muriel for many years, she insisted on adopting the child. Muriel was, indeed, a treasure. She brought sunshine into the lives of all who knew her, and when she developed a serious illness, it saddened her many friends. Though she possessed nothing of worldly value, her happiness and her beautiful smile, her interest in everything and everyone around her, endeared her to all.

With the approach of Christmas that year, as her illness worsened, we three children tried to think what we could give her as a present. We had been told that she would probably not live very much longer, but we could not believe it. Her huge eyes in her small white face were so bright and alive that we felt that death, for her, must be far off. We decided that she would still be able to read in her little bed under the sunny window, and thought a children's annual would be nice for her.

We slid our pennies out of our money-boxes with a knife (this was fairly easy and we often did it to count our riches) and we put them all together. There was a small but well-stocked shop at Quedgeley, two miles from our home. I tried to convince myself, my brother and sister that we could easily walk there and back before the early dark came down and said that I was sure we would find a book there. They half believed me, and, because it was necessary to do something quickly, they agreed to go to Quedgeley.

We set out in the half light of a December afternoon and reached our destination about three-quarters of an hour later. To our dismay the shop stocked no Children's Annuals. But the shopkeeper knew us and, as he was a very kind person, he went into his house and brought out a new book which he assured us would be just right for Muriel. It was to give her great happiness and, tired and late as we were and in disgrace with mother because of our lateness, we were all glad we had a book to give her for Christmas.

Our friend lived until the snowdrops and primroses opened in the spring sunshine and, after she died, we asked if we might look after her grave. There was nothing morbid about this. We — and later the other choir members — looked on the grave as our responsibility and keeping it clean and neat was a service performed for a loved friend. Muriel's family must have been very kind, to leave the care of their much-loved adopted sister's grave to children. They would have made a better job of it themselves, but were willing to leave it to her young friends. Though she had no worldy riches, Muriel left to her friends the treasure of having something that was our responsibility to care for and we gave all the love we could in return.

One of the sights with which we became very familiar was that of a small group of people, some eight or ten members of the same family, walking in the direction of St. Margaret's and carrying a baby dressed in a long white robe. A christening party almost always walked, carrying the baby. The baptism of a baby nearly caused a tragedy at our house once. Mother had promised to be Godmother to a friend's son and, as father was not at home, a neighbour said she would look in from time to time to see that we were all right. The baby's mother had been very ill, so, on this occasion, the walk was abandoned and a horse and trap took the small party to church.

Firewood was always dried in the oven of our range. Whether the oven became overheated, or whether we had pushed the wood too near the fire in reaching over the high fireguard, I cannot remember. But, suddenly, the whole oven and the dusters drying on the guard were alight. We were terrified, of course, and ran for Mrs Waite, the neighbour who had promised to 'look in'. She reached the scene just in time, and was able to throw all the burning material into the fire. We were never left alone again.

Weddings varied according to the wealth of the famililes concerned. Often the bridegroom and his family walked to church and it was more usual to see the bride dressed in a 'costume' (suit, today), wearing a hat and carrying a bunch of garden flowers, than one in a horse-drawn carriage. Carriages were used, but only very occasionally. As motor cars became more numerous, the wedding parties became grander. Films probably exercised their influence on both clothes and transport. We went to the cinema to watch a film occasionally and agonise over Pearl White in 'The Perils of Pauline' and, naturally, we imitated what we liked. Long dresses for weddings and proper transport both came into this category. So today's weddings, with long dresses, cars, bridesmaids and bouquets evolved over the years. The children eagerly watched all the wedding processions and discussed them at length for days afterwards.

Funerals were another matter. There was only one lane leading to the church — Grange Road — and along this most of the funerals passed. As it was considered bad form to watch the procession of mourners openly, everyone took advantage of the drawn blinds and curtains along the route. All the neighbours drew their curtains as a mark of respect, just as those in the street stood still as the cortege passed, and men doffed their caps and hats. So, although we watched from behind our drawn curtains, it was done respectfully and no one was observed watching. Funerals were always as grand as possible. Horses and carriages were always black and black ostrich plumes waved above the heads of the horses drawing the hearse. The chief male mourners often walked behind the hearse and behind them came a carriage bearing the ladies of the family. All were dressed in black, except small children who wore black armbands. The cortege walked all the way to the church, while the deep bell tolled for more than ten minutes. After the service in the church, most of the burials were in the churchyard, but occasionally the funeral procession went at walking pace all the way to the cemetery at Gloucester.

During and after World War I, military funerals used to pass our school on the way to St. Margaret's. We watched these openly if we were in the playground. The bands, the gun-carriage with its flag-draped coffin, usually with outriders, and sometimes, though not often, followed by women in carriages, all fascinated us. On the way to the church, the band played solemn, sombre music and the horses moved slowly and sedately, but we noticed that on the way back, the music was much jollier and the pace faster.

On warm days, when the doors were open during the services, the church was often visited by various animals. Cats wandered in and out; once a dog came in to see what was going on; birds frequently flew about high up in the roof, giving us an excuse to let our attention wander. The funniest visitor to come in one Sunday morning was a duck.

It waddled in during the singing of the psalm, quacking quietly as it came sedately up the aisle, turning its head from side to side and surveying each pew critically with its beady eyes, as if to make sure that everything was in its proper place. Advancing to the entrance to the chancel, it stopped and inspected the choir intently and then, apparently satisfied that all was as it should be, it turned and waddled sedately out again. The choir boys and girls nearly all lost their places, there was a great deal of nudging and sly grinning, until the vicar's pointed stare brought us back to consideration of what we really should be doing. Alas, we never saw that duck again.

Our country church typified the many others in which the torch of faith is still kept burning.

The annual Choir Outing was an event which was looked forward to eagerly by the choirs of both Brookthorpe and Whaddon churches. When we had enough funds, we hired a charabanc and were taken to Weston-super-Mare or the Cheddar Gorge, immensely enjoyable expeditions. If the year was a lean one, we cut our coat according to our cloth and made do with sports and a tea at the Vicarage at Brookthorpe. This kind of treat was very popular and we were joined there by the Sunday Schools. After a programme of energetic games and races, there was always a very good tea and everyone returned home tired but happy.

There is a complete list of incumbents, covering several hundred years, in Brookthorpe church. Four of them officiated while we and our contemporaries were growing up.

The Rev. Thomas Edgar Johnson and his wife came to the parish in 1916 and stayed nearly ten years. He was the vicar who discussed with my father the fate of the elm trees on the Green. When he left, there was quite a long gap before the next vicar arrived, but the interval was filled in the happiest possible way. Mr and Mrs Detmar Blow, who lived at Hilles House, high up on the Cotswolds, had their own resident priest for their private chapel, and when it became known that the sister churches were without a vicar, the Blows immediately offered the services of their 'Brother Michael'. Brother Michael was a delightful person, whose presence was accepted gratefully. He was, I believe, a Franciscan, and always wore a brown habit with a rope girdle. He used to walk all the way from Hilles House across the fields, a distance of quite four miles, making the journey in all kinds of weather, wearing only sandals on his feet and nothing to protect his habit. He must very often have been wet and cold, but in spite of this he always seemed happy and we enjoyed church services during the time that he came to take them.

Often it was dark as he set out on his long walk home, but nevertheless he always took a short cut across the corner of the Green to a small lane which led on to the hills. The Green was never without its hazards and darkness increased them. Brother Michael said of one dark night: 'I was walking home, doing no one any harm. It was pitch dark and suddenly my foot caught under something warm and the next thing I knew, I was draped over a huge warm heaving mound'. The mound was, of course, a cow. Such incidents were by no means rare, but falling over a cud-chewing cow in the dark can be very frightening. Fortunately, the cow was a gentle animal and neither she nor Brother Michael was any the worse for the encounter.

Our new vicar, the Rev. Edward Jones and his wife came in 1927. They were both very much loved. They worked unceasingly. As vicar, Mr Jones cycled countless miles visiting all his parishioners regularly. He had a wonderful sense of humour and was an excellent mimic. We all welcomed his visits. He was, however, a strict disciplinarian and it was he who stopped us gossiping and amusing ourselves in church simply by breaking off whatever he happened to be saying and staring hard at the culprit. He brought new life to the churches and then, suddenly, at the end of his first year in office, he died, leaving the parishes bereft.

1928 saw the induction of David Hedog-Jones. Like his predecessor, he was a Welshman, but there all resemblance ended. Anyone would have had an uphill road to travel after our beloved Edward. The Rev. David's approach was very different from that of his predecessor. He had been a missionary in a poor part of Africa, where the swampy ground gave mosquitos plenty of encouragement and malaria was widespread. In those days, there was no cure for this dreadful illness and our new vicar was prone to suffer very bad attacks, from which he never fully recovered.

Having lived in what is now known as the Third World, he was scandalised by our wastefulness and the way we accepted what he saw as luxuries, when so much of the world was starving. He expounded his views from the pulpit. Apparently not only were we rich and wasteful, but, in addition, our country refused to pay the just and proper price for goods sent from Africa, with the result that whole cargoes were dumped in the sea, adding to the distress of an already poor country.

There were dark mutterings among his flock, who had never accepted him as they had accepted Mr Edward Jones. We said he ought not to bring politics into the pulpit. Over the years, a dwindling congregation gradually got the message and came to realise that we are all members of one world and those who are richer have a duty to share their goods, money and ideas with their poorer brothers. But his principles were never accepted wholeheartedly at that time. Many years were to pass before society, in general, recognised the oneness of the world and acknowledged the moral obligations of wealthier nations towards the developing countries. David must often have been unhappy and insecure.

The Rev. Thomas Jenkyns came to us in 1938. He had a gentler manner than David and his congregation listened to him with much less discomfort.

The period of his incumbency was no easy time. Many were abandoning the traditional churches. Then, when World War II broke out, in September 1939, all the fit men joined the forces and the older ones and those less fit were drafted into other war work. Home Guard and Air Raid Warden's duties occupied most evenings for all those still at home. The boundaries of Gloucester City were extended and Tuffley had its own church. Whaddon and Brookthorpe were joined as one village — Brookthorpe with Whaddon.

The effect of the two world wars was to turn the parish into what Elizabeth Vowles describes as 'the village of the Amazons' .. She adds, 'nearly all the drive of the community came from women'. Among those who bravely kept the churches and the parish going were Mrs Maitland, Village Hall Chairman and Lord of Brookthorpe Manor, Miss Forssman, Chairman of the Parish Council, Mrs Castle, the village's unofficial Social Worker and, later, W. I. Secretary and a District Councillor of a quality not often seen, and Dorothy Thomas. Now, says Mrs Vowles, the wheel had turned full circle. After a great effort had been made to get a woman on the Parish Council, that woman was going off to America and it scarcely looked as if another would be found. However, it was good to know that the men were back.

Even now, when they are poor themselves, the two churches still help the needy of the parish, pooling their resources. The hundred pounds a year, which is all that they can spare, is generally used to help pay fuel or light bills. The Trustees are responsible to the Parish Council.

The changes of the last half century have left the parish disjointed, with three different types of inhabitant — the old residents, now very few, the commuters, and the council house tenants. Brookthorpe with Whaddon needs time to adjust.

Before ending this chapter, in somewhat lighter vein, another change must be touched on: Church-going clothes were often more old fashioned than those worn every day before the Second War, Best clothes were kept for going to church, and were put away carefully after church until the next Sunday, so they lasted a very long time. Clothes which had started as black often turned faintly green or rust coloured. Older ladies kept the grandeur of Edwardian outfits well into the 1920s.

Hats were made of various materials and in various styles, ranging from toques to ones with large brims. Many had veils and a vast quantity of trimming of all sorts was stitched on to them. Flowers, in wreaths or singly, ribbon, artificial fruit — especially cherries — feathers and, sometimes, whole humming birds could be admired during the church service. One veil, worn by Mrs Johnson, the vicar's wife, was a particularly splendid one of thick silk, which covered her face completely and was tied up at the back. Neck bands, called chokers, were made of velvet ribbon and usually had some ornament fixed at the front. Hats required hatpins, perched as they often were on top of large buns of hair.

Two dear ladies who were great supporters of St. Margaret's until they died, aged over eighty, were Mrs Brown and Miss Bayliss. They lived in Grange Road and walked the mile and a half to church and back all their lives, until they became too ill to do so any longer. Their hatpins were very much in evidence. Those of Mrs Brown caused us great concern, because they were set so close together that it seemed they must actually go through her head. Straw hats were refurbished from time to time and all trimmings were changed. The Second World War finally established shorter hair for the majority of women and hats 'went out', except for very special occasions, or to give warmth in winter.

Children still enjoy studying the gravestones and Mrs Vowles sometimes has them in her home, plying her with questions about the families represented by them. Recently some children she talked to returned later and showed her a huge genealogical table of members of one family that they had made. Many people make regular pilgrimages to the churchyards. Among the visitors at Whaddon was one old lady who returned every year from her home 'up North', to visit the grave of a child who had died aged two and a half years. This was her elder sister. She must have been too young when this happened to remember her, but she brought exquisite little bouquets to leave on the grave. Possibly it was the last link she had with her childhood, a root to which she was irresistably drawn back.

St. Margaret's Church, Whaddon.

Chapter Eleven   Progress

Between World Wars I and II, Lower Tuffley was given constant attention and grooming by the powers which control all modern amenities such as gas, electricity, city water and sewerage, which brought the village into line with modernisation in other parts of Gloucestershire.

Gas was the first to come and the trenches dug to take the gas mains made the lanes even narrower than they were before. But the trenches dug for gas mains were as nothing compared with those which were needed for laying on city water, while the sewage mains, which must have a continuous, gradual fall, demanded huge trenches, very deep in places, which took up a great deal of space. There were no red and green traffic lights in those days; travellers had to look ahead as far as was possible, and if they could not see, they just had to hope that no other vehicle would approach the part of the road they had to traverse. The lives of all tradesmen and the post lady were made very difficult for a number of years. It was not only the main trench they had to cope with; smaller ones went to each house which had to be negotiated carefully. As most tradesmen started deliveries very early, a lot of coping was done in the dark during all except summer mornings.

116

In spite of the inconvenience caused, we were very grateful for all the improvements. Gas made cleaning and filling oil lamps and polishing and replenishing candlesticks unnecessary, and it was much simpler to cook a meal on a gas stove, where the heat was more easily controlled, than in a range and much cleaner as well. One thing the children discovered was that cakes could be spoilt more easily in a gas oven by slamming the door, than in the oven of the range, which was surrounded by heat flues, so that the temperature did not drop as sharply when the door was opened and closed quickly. We found that opening and shutting the gas oven door made a cake 'flat', it did not rise, and our mothers, thinking they were to blame through not being used to cooking by gas, would make another cake and let us eat the 'flat' one. This went on until one Mum found out the truth, and she promptly spread the word. Our days of lots of flat cakes were over.

After gas came water and sewerage. They really were great blessings. The wells in the village often went dry in the summer when the rainfall was low and some people had to trudge to get water from a deep well in the Colonel's orchard. During the dry summers of 1921 and 1929, a water cart went round the village each day and we queued up with our buckets and tin baths. I remember standing by our pails waiting to have them filled, though I did not carry them back full. We were allowed only about two buckets full for each house, so we found it a blessing that our well was filled by spring water, not surface water. Even so, my father took the cart, full of milk churns, over three fields to fill them from the Sandfords brook, so that there would be enough water to sterilise the milk utensils.

Imagine the joy of just turning a tap and seeing water come out with no need to pump up a tankful first! It was luxury. So was sewerage when that was laid on. It had been a constant struggle to keep our earth closets clean and sweet smelling—the latter being nearly impossible. To have a toilet that one was able simply to flush clean was bliss indeed. No more emptying of cesspools! The disappearance of the old closets, however, had one unforeseen result. It deprived youngsters of the chance of saying something we thought very funny. Every Christmas, and at parties, we played a certain game called 'Consequences'. This involved writing down answers to a series of questions. When you had written down your answer to a question, you folded the paper over and passed it on to your neighbour to answer the next one, and so on. The questions ran something like this: What was his name? What was her name? Where did they meet? What did he say? What did she say? The consequences were -? Our papers almost invariably said they met 'in the two-seater', and the reference was not to a car! Our closets, built many years earlier, often had two or more seats; sometimes there was also a small one for a child. Our ancestors must have been less fussy about privacy than we are! Having proper toilets spoilt all that. All the same, they were a great blessing and made a vast difference to a rural community such as ours.

The last of the modern improvements to come to our village was electricity. This made an enormous difference to our lives. We had got used to hissing gas brackets, but to get light at the touch of a switch, heat in any room where one wanted it, power to drive a 'fridge' and other farming machinery such as milking machines — this was luxury to us. No one born after the 1940s will ever realise how much people's lives changed in just three decades.

People began to be more organised. Boy Scout and Girl Guide movements were popular and boys and girls learned in them a multitude of crafts and became proficient in skills like swimming, especially life saving, all kinds of camping crafts, first aid, and so on, while at the same time enjoying it. They had to be able to accept discipline in order to expand their capabilities. Guides and (on occasions) Scouts met in the Colonel's loft, which was next to ours and we listened enviously (being still too young to join in) to the fun and games and the pounding feet on the board floor of the loft next door.

The Grange was an ideal meeting place for, as well as the loft, there was a large horseshoe-shaped lawn, which was the very thing for outdoor functions. I still recollect a sort of exhibition of which Carew writes, 'I remember we (the Guides) had some sort of display in July 1921; camp cooking in the orchard, and a play on the lawn in which I had to recite Kipling's 'If'. Of plays, she says, 'later on we used to act our own when our cousins, the Beans, came in the summer holidays. 'Aldobrandini, the Brigand' was the first play'. Acting was very tricky, because from time to time the noise of passing trains would drown people's voices, and the extended lines of freight or goods waggons could take an awfully long time to go by! A great deal of miming to fill in was necessary. Sometimes these trains came to a complete standstill on the steep gradient and then one had to shout above the sound of hissing steam, until a relief engine came from Gloucester to boost the power needed to move the stranded waggons. Why two engines were not attached in the first place, we never knew.

The money raised by such performances as those done by the Guides always went to some current good cause. The plays written and acted at the Grange were the inspiration needed by the village youngsters to make them write and act their own plays, as groups in the village. As we grew older, we learnt to produce whole concerts, with plays, singing and dancing, much of which was composed by ourselves. We had, at that time, no local village hall, but used either someone's garden, the Red Cross Room, Whaddon Church Hall or the Y.M.C.A. huts (all now demolished). Always the money raised was given to the most pressing good cause of the time.

Another of the enlighted organisations to be introduced in the 1920s was the Women's Institute. My mother's help was enlisted in making people aware that a branch of the Women's Institute was to be opened for the whole of Tuffley—Upper and Lower—as well as for Whaddon. It was to be called 'Tuffley and Whaddon Women's Institute', with meetings to be held in the Red Cross Room each month. Carew has told me that her stepmother was always deeply interested in the movement which claimed many of the village women as members. Far from being 'all jam and Jerusalem', the W.I. was the chief instigator of Women's Lib. in the 1920s. The Institute's motto was 'Service, not Self', and it was a real service to all who came into contact with it. Women learned that there was more to life than continual drudgery. Emancipation came to the villages with the W.I.; lectures and demonstrations on developing everything, beginning with people's own sense of values, their personalities, talking things out together, learning all sorts of crafts, hearing about travel, voyages and experiences of all kinds. The members formed choirs and drama groups; they took part in games and competitions. The Institutes were among the greatest blessings countrywomen have ever known. Among other things, mother learned how to do upholstery and promptly upholstered four of our sitting room chairs—very well, too.

Although television now brings all these things into our homes, people can only watch and listen. The third thing necessary—participation—is missing, so it is a very one-way affair. The W.I. brought 'do-it-yourself' up to a very high level. The members *did* make jam, and jolly glad we were of it during World War II; and they did sing 'Jerusalem', and we all learnt more about William Blake in consequence, as well as turning our minds to questions about what our Jerusalem here was really like. Mind you, it wasn't perfect. The W.I. has its drawbacks. Mother, for instance, took up poetry reading and reciting and many were the times I had to stand near her, holding her poetry book and hear her memorising her lines, while she scrubbed a floor or polished furniture. Poor dear! she had not the time to set aside just for learning poetry.

One thing mother learned very well—a woman ought to have her own housekeeping money. Until then, father had always taken a list of her wants and, as he was in Gloucester every day, he did the shopping. If there were things he did not think it necessary for us to have, he just forgot them. Mother and all the W.I. members now became aware that they had a right to a part of what came into a house to spend as seemed good to them. There were many bitter arguments over housekeeping money when we were young, but, in the end, the women got their way and receiving housekeeping money became part of life.

A branch of the Young Men's Christian Association was started in Tuffley during the 1920s, when two large huts were erected on the Stroud road as a memorial to those who died in World War I. They were to be used by young Christians of Tuffley (Lower and Upper) and Whaddon. A great deal of money was needed to pay for them and all sorts of activities took place to raise funds. Fetes, which included vegetable and flower shows, were held on the football field behind Whaddon School. Diana remembers that one year there was a slippery pole, which must have been decidedly dangerous, since there was no water under it to break the impact of a fall.

Much discussion and preliminary work took place, with many of the men of the village being involved. My father became a committee member. When the huts were finished, Mr Money of Wyndyates — a large square house which stood nearby — was manager and caretaker. The huts contained full-sized billiard tables, concert platforms with large dressing rooms, which also served as kitchens, tables for whist, and enough games to keep people fully occupied in their spare time. The Y.M.C.A. gave the men of our villages plenty of scope for enjoyment.

Tuffley had both football and cricket teams, with grounds for them to play on. The football ground, next to the school, was very level and was kept well rolled. The cricket pitch, however, could be difficult. There was a steep drop behind one wicket and bowlers gradually disappeared from sight as they marked out their run-up, reappearing suddenly over the brow, hurling the ball overarm down the wicket as they did so. Brawny fellows our bowlers were, too. Timid batsmen stood no chance against them. Every match was an adventure, after which the teams went back to the Y.M.C.A. huts, tired but happy.

In addition to providing leisure activities, the Y.M.C.A. raised funds to care for those in need in the parish. Raffles, whist drives, concerts — you name it, they did it, and many people who might have been very poor indeed, in times when State aid came only after everything of value and considered dispensable had been sold, benefitted greatly and in complete secrecy. The secrecy often attracted criticism, but my father told me that sometimes the committee, when they had not quite enough money to purchase some particular article that was needed (money could not be given, otherwise any official aid coming in would be stopped), would dip into their own pockets to make up the deficit. The only people who knew exactly what was given were the committee and the recipients. There was still little work to be obtained in our village, and it had to be sought elsewhere. This meant that our young people went to Gloucester and even further afield to find work and they often married folk in the area of their employment. Those who remained were growing older and there were few young ones to follow them.

Until the bicycle became a popular means of transport, people generally walked from place to place and the footpaths marked the shortest routes from home to work or town. As our group of youngsters neared their teens, money was a little more plentiful, the country gradually recovered from the shortage of jobs, and many people learned to ride bicycles.

Father bought us a bike to share between us, so that we could all learn to ride. He had already given mother one. Hers was a very tall model and when mounted, she looked almost as if she was standing up. She rode with arms stiff and straight, looking directly ahead, a really imposing figure! She must have had that cycle all of twenty years, because even in the Second War she rode it for miles to a cafe where she sometimes had a meal in order to save the rations.

Ours was a much lower and tougher model. My sister, Naomi, was away from home when we were given our bike, so my brother and I learned first. Of course, we quarrelled about sharing it and I remember joining some friends and beginning on their bicycle, which had a fixed wheel. The method of teaching we used among ourselves was simple and hair-raising. The victim was settled on the machine, feet on the pedals, hands on the handlebars and seat on the saddle (if one could reach the saddle). The bicycle would then be taken to the top of a slope—usually steep—and given a vigorous shove. The unfortunate learner generally wobbled violently from side to side, shrieking all the time, while the cycle gathered speed. The rider stayed on until he or she became too terrified to balance and fell over. If one had a machine with a 'fixed wheel' (which meant that there was no possibility of freewheeling as the speed increased), one just had to go on pedalling faster and faster. No matter how quickly it went, there was no let up. As the cycle I first rode had a fixed wheel, this nightmare happened to me.

The first three times I tried, I landed up on the grass verge, with the bicycle on top of me and its oily chain all over me. (Very popular-making with those who had to help us clean up afterwards). The brakes never seemed to come to hand at the right time, one became more and more tense and rigid, while all the previous good advice on how to stop vanished from one's memory. The beginner was too terrified to think of anything except keeping upright on the bike, so it just went on gathering momentum, until it ended up in a hedge or a ditch.

My brother Eric learned with his boy friends, so I was not around to laugh at his mishaps. Naomi returned home, having recuperated from her illness, all excitement about learning to ride a bike. We had been warned to take special care of her since she had been ill, so we held her up while we pushed the bike for some time. Eventually we grew tired of pushing and decided that, invalid or not, Naomi would have the learn the same way as everyone else did.

The first time on her own she wobbled about and finally landed in a blackberry bush, getting scratched all over. However, she was nothing if not a tryer. At her second attempt by herself, she kept the machine upright, though it gained speed rapidly. It carried on past the open lane to where the houses began, still going at speed. We shouted to her to put the brakes on, but panic had seized my sister. 'I can't stop, I can't stop', she cried repeatedly. We yelled all the more about the brakes, but to no avail. The cycle kept on going. As she neared the houses, inspiration came to her. She turned the handlebars in the direction we always went for help—Mr and Mrs Haine's front door! Ivetsey Cottage bordered the road, so no front garden impeded her progress. Coming to the door to find out what all the commotion was about, Ernie Haines opened it just in time to admit Naomi, bike and all. Tea was laid, and the Hainses had been sitting quietly, enjoying a few minutes chat until the interruption occurred.

Still in the saddle, clinging frantically to the handlebars, Naomi careered into the table, upsetting everything. Mr and Mrs Haines's quiet interlude was rudely shattered, along with a quantity of crockery.

After the initial shock, Mrs Haines laid aside her own confusion in an effort to comfort Naomi, while Ernie, her husband, set about the business of separating my sister from the bike. Mrs Haines was someone we could always go to for comfort, no matter what the circumstances. She never failed us. Likewise, her husband always mended our punctured or buckled bikes; so he got down to straightening this one. Neither of them ever told our parents about our escapades, although we must frequently have caused them quite a bit of trouble. They were wonderful friends. They often had children staying with them for holidays or recuperating from some illness. Occasionally they gave us lovely teas. For all their kindness they asked nothing in return except our friendship.

In addition, to compensate for having no family of their own, they always kept one dog—sometimes two—and several cats, all of which they took for walks. We would often see them walking arm in arm and surrounded by their pets in the country lanes on a summer evening.

In time we were all able to ride and then the village children resorted to hair-raising stunts: 'Look, no hands!', riding with feet and hands free, with one foot on the handlebars, or sitting on the handlebars with feet on the saddle. Our lanes were still very quiet (although they ran in a succession of steep little rises and dips), so our behaviour was not as dangerous as it would be today.

After seeing us ride, one on the handlebars, one on the saddle and one on the carrier behind, our parents thought it was high time we had a bicycle each.

Perhaps they were influenced, too, by the fact that during one summer holiday I had conceived the idea of building a bicycle and riding it. I found some wooden wheels and I only had wood from which to construct the rest of it; but build it I did. It had no pedals, so I paddled my feet on the ground, for the brief space of time it hung together. The contraption actually travelled the length of the drive before falling apart.

When we and many of the other village youngsters all had cycles, we went for marvellous rides. Our horizons expanded all the time. We went up to the Horsepools (pushing our bikes), down the other side into Stroud (no brakes and see who can go the fastest!), through the town, finding our way as we went, then home via Eastington, Hardwick and Quedgeley — all places on the busy Bristol road. We must have helped to turn our parents' hair white. All this was done in groups of eight or ten young people. Going downhill, we used to swing our legs to urge our machines on to ever greater speeds. We often had to walk uphill.

Bicycles made it possible to visit local places which were beyond walking distance — Elmore, for instance, to see the Severn Bore, a great wall of water which comes up the river twice a day in spring. During the Easter holidays, the village children used to cycle the four or five miles to Elmore, going as close to the river as they dared. Often the surrounding fields and roads were flooded and one of my sister's friends, who lived at Elmore, frequently had to sit on a stile when on her way home and wait for the tide to go down.

The Bore can be heard approaching for some distance away. When there are no obstacles, water flows in a straight line, but the Severn turns and twists and as the wave hit the banks on the bends, we could hear it crashing on them as well as the thunder of its approach. We loved watching the Bore, that seething, noisy, boiling mass of muddy water that, every year, people try to ride either in boats or on surfboards. It is very hazardous, no doubt, but I expect they get as much enjoyment from doing it as we did from riding our bikes dangerously. During the 20s and 30s, people still lived in these areas that got flooded each year and even later when mother was dying and we wanted the District Nurse, she was unable to come because she was helping an old lady who had been trapped, sitting in icy water up to her knees.

When the river levelled up, it would be many feet deeper than it had been before the Bore came along; then, in great patches on the muddy water, there would be thousands and thousands of elvers, tiny eels, returning to the river from the open sea. Fishermen went out to catch them in long-handled nets. They dipped the nets into the water and brought out many pounds of the wriggling elvers, which were then put into baths or clothes baskets lined with sheets. Later they were hawked round the villages in prams or wheelbarrows. The fishermen kept up a call of 'Elvers, elvers'. Sometimes they rang a handbell. The elvers were measured out in pint measures, and cost sixpence a pint. Today they are all bought by a factory and canned, so that it is only rarely that local people can buy them. The cost has gone up considerably, too.

They should be washed thoroughly before cooking. They are then put into a frying pan over heat either in butter or with beaten egg poured over them. Those who eat them say they are delicious, but I have never been able to bring myself to sample them.

Newent and Dymock, where wild daffodils grew, were two other places we used to cycle to in spring. We would set off early on the eleven mile ride. It seemed a long way, but the journey was always worthwhile and tremendous fun. As one approached Newent, daffodils began to appear in the hedges and in the grass of the fields. Some fields were yellow with them, and just to see them filled us with excitement. We continued on our way until we reached what we thought were the largest flowers, which often were growing in the woods. People less privileged than we were then can never know the sense of elation we felt as we stood surrounded by thousands of flowers. In the woods, they were about a foot high and the trees seemed to rise up out of a sea of gold. We picked and picked, making up bunches as we went until the handlebars of our bicycles would hold no more. Then we returned home, reaching the village in the gathering dusk, tired and happy, with our minds full of the vivid memory of that wonderful sight, fields and woods carpeted with golden daffodils. The next day we took bunches to all our friends and people who were sick, keeping only one bunch each for ourselves. Nearly every house in the village would have a bunch of daffodils in the spring.

The joy this outing gave us was beyond imagining and, when I grew older and was offered a job selling ice-cream in Eastgate Market on Saturday afternoons, father just could not understand why I should turn down the good money that went with it, simply to cycle to Newent and pick daffodils. They still grow in the woods and fields of Newent, but today people have to pay quite a lot of money for permission to pick just a few. Indeed, this is a wise precaution, since with the great number of cars and many more people visiting the district, it would be all too easy to exterminate these lovely flowers.

In the course of growing up I owned two bicycles, both very dear to me for different reasons. One was a beautiful Raleigh sports model, which took me on rides all over Gloucestershire and the surrounding counties in the company of the Gloucester City Cycling Club. The other was a machine with no pedigree, attached to a chassis which carried a frame built to hold bottles of milk, boxes of eggs, butter and cream. This bicycle was my constant companion during the latter part of my life at Lower Tuffley. Together this combination and I conveyed thousands of gallons of milk to an estate which had mushroomed near our home, and people looking for me found me by looking for my bicycle.

The motor car began to be seen in the village not long after the bicycle had found a place in the homes of most Lower Tuffley families. Tradespeople were the first to invest in motor vehicles, as they found they were speedier and able to carry heavier loads than horses did. There were not many privately owned cars. Even Colonel Sinnott, with his responsible position as County Surveyor, pedalled to and from his work at the Shire Hall on his bicycle. Later on he did make a certain concession to 'progress' by having a motorised unit attached to the rear of his machine, thus giving it extra power, and he continued quite happily like this until in the 1920s an official car, with chauffeur, was put at his service.

My father would not consider having a van or car until the later 1930s, when Tommy grew too old to work. Although he tried several other horses, none of them gave him—or us—the same pleasure as Old Tom. So eventually he bought a motor bike, with one sidecar fitted to take his stock-in-trade and another to use when going for outings. The first motor bike was not a success. It never went properly and we seemed to spend as much time pushing it as it did travelling under its own power. It must be admitted that this was partly due to inexpert handling, and partly to the fact that engines were much less reliable in those days than they are today. He certainly provided many laughs as he shouted at it to 'WHOA', or 'COME ON, WILL YOU!'. The horses had always obeyed him and it took him a long time to realise that he had to be the directing power behind an automobile.

Sometimes he exasperated us, sometimes we laughed, but no one laughed when one day he announced that he and mother and Eric were going to drive to Bath to meet an uncle and aunt who were staying there. He said they would take the motor bike with dad driving, mother in the sidecar, and Eric riding pillion (Eric was always good with machinery and they needed him in case of engine trouble).

When the day arrived, I watched as dad drove the machine gingerly round the bend in the drive and headed for the Bristol road. Eric looked particularly smart in a new school blazer and cap. His old cap had endured many vicissitudes; all the boys hated them and they kicked them around until they were in a disgraceful condition. Before they started, I heard mother say, 'Now you have a new cap, we expect you to take care of it. If you reduce this cap to the state of the last one, there will be trouble!'.

I passed the day coping with the usual tasks — washing and sterilizing the milk utensils, watering and feeding the horses, pigs and poultry, until I finished everything about seven and went into the house to change and prepare a meal for the travellers.

I switched on the wireless, which was a cat's whiskers affair. It was a small box which contained a large black crystal. At the front of the covering glass was a switch, which controlled a long, thin, whisker-like piece of wire. When you wished to 'listen-in', you put on headphones and tickled the crystal with this whisker, until suddenly there was a blast of noise, which, by use of a modulating control, was gradually converted into words, singing or music coming from London. The young and middle-aged of today can hardly realise what a sense of awe and wonderment those strange, somewhat distorted sounds, frequently obliterated by oscillation, brought to us in those early days of broadcasting. We had two sets of headphones for our wireless which we had to share, and when someone was listening, everyone else was expected to be quiet.

My brother, as the up-and-coming mechanic, was never entirely satisfied with the reception obtained by someone else, so, just as one was becoming interested in a programme, often a horrible, screeching noise told us that he was trying to do better. Sometimes, as he jiggled the switch about, the sound did improve, but Eric was never really satisfied that it was as good as it should be.

That evening I listened in peace until night came down and it was time to switch on the light. Ten o'clock came and went, but still there was no sound of the chugging of the engine that I waited for. At last, about ten thirty I heard it, growing louder as the motor bike came up the drive and then stopped in the yard. Father, mother and Eric came in, looking very tired and strangely dirty. They did not want supper at once, but went off to wash. I thought, 'Oh well, it was quite a journey, they'll need to freshen up'.

When eventually they sat down to supper, they seemed unusually subdued and when I asked them about their day out, they replied in monosyllables. 'How did you get on?' I said. 'All right', was the answer — nothing more. Questioned about aunt and uncle, they said they hadn't had long to see them. I thought, 'That's funny, Bath is only thirty miles away'. The motor cycle frequently travelled at thirty miles an hour. They were very tired and still looked grubby, so I made no further comment and we talked about the milk and the animals.

A day or two later, I saw Eric's new cap. It was stained with large patches of black oil and covered with small black holes, as if it had been burnt by sparks from a bonfire. I asked, 'Whatever happened to your cap, Eric?' 'Mind your own business', he replied rudely and with finality. 'Well', I thought, 'it can only be a matter of days before mum and dad find out'. He must have worn it to go to school, although it looked so disreputable. The days passed, however, and finally I gave up expecting trouble over the cap. The motor bike went for an overhaul, but as it seemed to spend its time in and out of the garage, I thought nothing of it.

One day, a little later, I saw mother washing the cap. She said something like, 'What a shame about that cap'. 'What happened to it?' I asked. Then, at last, she told me. 'On the way to Bath, one of the cylinders of the motor bike went on fire and Eric really saved our lives by leaning over and smotherng the flames with his cap'. It hadn't put the fire out completely, but a passing AA man used his fire extinguisher on the blaze and finally doused it. She told me they had had to push the motor bike a long way to the nearest garage and wait while it was repaired. No wonder they had not grumbled. Had it not been for Eric's prompt action, they could well have been badly burned and the bike would certainly have been a write-off. After their long journey and the wait they had had while the machine was being repaired, there was only half an hour left to see their relatives. The cap was never any use again. Father's opinion of automobiles, never very high, went down several notches, and the AA gained a new member.

Chapter Twelve   'Coming Events Cast Their Shadows Before'

(Thomas Campbell)

As we and our friends grew up, it seemed that the village grew up too. After so many years when conditions were primitive, Lower Tuffley has developed into a place where modern amenities made living much more pleasant. No houses were built except for filling in gaps in the existing rows. Some of the modern houses were erected where old wells still remained, showing that dwellings had been on those sites previously.

Confirmation seemed to be the dividing line for the village children between childhood and young adulthood. Most of us were confirmed as Christians in the Church of England about the age of fourteen, after which we began to enjoy more grown-up occupations and recreations. Most young people were expected to help with the work of their homes and gardens and the girls learnt to make some of their own clothes. During hard times, it is much easier for rural communities to bridge the gaps than it is for people living in towns.

My sister and I learned to do intricate embroidery and when a good magazine on needlework was published, we bought copies for sixpence each. Colour printing was emerging, making the pictures much more interesting than they had been in black and white, and the work was easier to follow. We made tablecloths, embroidered sheets, pillowslips, towels, and, what we liked best, pictures of symbolic trees, though I did not realise until recently, when an old friend passed on the information, that the exotic birds, fruit and flowers on the trees represented the life stories of real people. These tree pictures originated at the time of the Crusades, when the knights brought back to their homes silks from the East, and their ladies designed and worked them. Each bird, fruit and flower represented some event in their lives. The articles we made and embroidered served as presents for our friends and also provided us with great interest. Clark's Anchor stranded cotton cost twopence a skein and, if one needed 40 different colours for a piece of work the cost was still under ten shillings (there were 240 pence to the £1 then). Irish linen and twill could be purchased at most good drapers at around £1 for a piece of material 48 inches square. So although we had far less money to spend, it went a good deal further than it would today.

When we were 15 and 16, my sister and I were allowed to go on holiday to Weston-Super-Mare together. We enjoyed most of it enormously, but the evening before we were due to return home, as we sat on the promenade, a storm blew up. I wanted to finish a piece of embroidery, but my sister has always been terrified of thunder and begged me to go home with her. I selfishly continued my work until it was almost raining and we had to run back to our digs.

About this time, we were also allowed to go to local dances, held in surrounding halls and schools. These dances were organised on behalf of charities, and everyone got a great deal of fun out of them. Moreover the preparation for these occasions was as much appreciated as the actual entertainment itself. We spent hours washing, creaming and 'making-up'. Our powder was pinky, so were our silk stockings, while lipstick was usually a rather harsh bright red. All the girls used a great deal of perfume of the Soir de Paris and Shem el Nessim varieties. The combined effect of heavily perfumed females, charging round in an overheated, confined space, became almost overpowering. Not that the boys were behind in the perfume game. They wore lots of scented brilliantine (after-shave lotion had not been invented then) and the combination of the girls' perfume and the men's brilliantine gave many couples a good excuse to go outside for a breather. Funnily enough, no one seemed to take cold from going out of a hot room into the cool night air.

Before these dances began, the floors were liberally dusted with either boracic crystals or French chalk and, as the evening progressed, the floor became more and more slippery, while the air got thick with powder and cigarette smoke. These floors were often knotty and uneven, but the hazards only added to the fun. We reckoned to dance every dance and if two girls were sitting out, they danced together. There was generally the 'three-piece band' — piano, drums and either violin or saxophone, for it was the age of jazz.

The best dance hall we had locally was built under the direction of Mr Whitfield, who managed the brickworks until they closed. When the kilns were no longer needed for baking bricks, the dance hall was built above them. We enjoyed dancing on its beautifully level and polished floor and having all the amenities of a purpose-made room — until those responsible for fire precautions deemed it too dangerous. There was only one wooden stairway up to the room and, had there been a fire, many accidents could have resulted. Mr Whitfield must have been bitterly disappointed, great trouble had been taken to make the hall acceptable and fire extinguishers were prominently displayed. Nevertheless, the hall had to be closed.

Occasionally there was high-spirited horseplay, but we never experienced the vicious behaviour of these days. No intoxicating drinks were allowed and if anyone was suspected of having been drinking, he was not admitted. We have a family joke which stemmed from one of these dances. My sister, dancing in a Paul Jones, was unfortunate enough to stop opposite a boy whose exuberance far exceeded his skill in dancing. She gamely put up with his antics until the dance ended and we made ladies and gentlemen's rings once more. When the music stopped the next time, Naomi had a much quieter partner and, beginning to feel more secure, she began to tell him about the other boy. Her observations were not very flattering and her new partner, after listening for a time, became very red in the face and burst out with, 'Excuse me, that's my pal!' For years after, if either was in a similar position, the obvious reply would be, 'Excuse me, that's my pal!'

Most people knew each other and a group of us would usually walk to our homes together, often a distance of some miles. We girls sometimes walked without our shoes, because our feet had become so swollen that when we took off our evening shoes, we could not get our day shoes on! We generally sang all the way. There seemed to be so many songs we all knew then. Most of the dance tunes had lyrics and we learned the words as we sang round our pianos when we had friends at home in the evenings.

The cinema formed an important part of the weekly entertainment, although films were still silent for a year or two yet. Some of them were in serial form and finished abruptly with the heroine left tied to a railway track, while the oncoming train appeared in the distance, or pinned against a wall by a villain with a knife. We *had* to go the following week to see what happened to the poor girl. (Those serials were a good way of ensuring that most people came back again).

The pianists who played for the film were most remarkable people. They just played on and on, suiting the music to the mood of the film, all the while in almost total darkness. In Gloucester there was one pianist who played at two cinemas, dashing from one to the other in turn. Some items, such as the advertisements, did not seem to need music, but, even so, a great deal of good organisation must have been needed to get the pianist to the right place at the right time. There were three complete programmes each day, so the pianists must have been exhausted by the end of the week.

When 'talkies' first came, my sister and I saw Al Jolsen in 'The Singing Fool'. We thought it wonderful. We could not have imagined a time when there would be no more ballads, and pop groups would sing songs which the audience could not hear because of the noise of the accompanying musical instruments.

We were soon going to places of entertainment with our separate friends and the funniest film I ever saw was 'The Desert Song', to which I was taken by a boyfriend. It was supposed to be highly romantic; the story was about a handsome desert sheik who carried off an English girl, whom, of course, he married in the end. Unfortunately, the sound track was out of time with the film, so that when the hero was talking passionately, no sound came over, while, when silence was supposed to be absolute, a whole spate of words came cascading over the audience. We laughed all the way through the film, but had to sit through the programme twice in order to get the gist of it, and get the appropriate words linked with the action.

The Mighty Wurlitzers were popular then and their day lasted nearly twenty years. These were huge electric organs, which descended into the pit in front of the screen. When it was time for a recital, they rose slowly and spectacularly, with the organist playing, until they were in full view and a spotlight focussed on the musician in charge. These organs had stops representing every known instrument, plus some extra noises, so the organists at their keyboards had to be highly competent musicians. They were literally in charge of a complete orchestra. When television became cheap enough for most people to own a set, the organs and the organists, and even many of the cinemas themselves, quietly faded away.

Most young people played tennis sometimes, on the public courts on the Stroud road, and most of us swam, either in the Public Baths or in the Canal. The boys swam there most summer evenings; they fished there too. The boys had their separate hobbies, such as cricket and football, which the girls went along to watch. The teams were always looking for supporters. They also bought air guns and, when they were older, rifles, which they used for shooting rabbits. My brother and his friend, Alban, went out shooting about twice a week. Sometimes the hayricks standing in the fields became the home of many rats and rabbits. The farmers were glad to get the vermin reduced, and willingly gave the boys permission to shoot.

One evening, while out looking for rabbits, the boys noticed a certain hayrick, about ten foot high, of which only one corner remained uncut. To their amazement it appeared to be shaking violently. Unthinkingly one of them fired into it. Out fell two figures, a boy and a girl, who made off as fast as their legs could carry them. For a minute or two, Alban and Eric remained petrified, realising only too well that their thoughtlessness could have resulted in someone being badly hurt. Then, having recovered from their fright, they sat down and laughed and laughed.

The evening Eric shot a wild duck wasn't funny at all. Colonel Sinnott kept several pairs of wild duck on the ponds in his orchards and during the daytime they often flew over the village, returning to their home as dusk fell. One evening, seeing what he thought were real wild duck flying overhead, Eric shot before he thought about it and unfortunately his aim was good. One of the ducks fell dead. Too late he realised his mistake. He and Naomi took it to show the Colonel later that evening and Eric said how sorry he was. The Colonel's reply was short and sad. 'I am sorry, too', he said. 'Be more careful next time'.

Alban's main hobby was keeping pigeons. He had a large flock of his own and learned a great deal about managing them. He taught the younger boys about ringing the birds and when tired pigeons alighted on the village roofs, it was Alban they turned to for help. He would either manage to reach the birds or entice them down so that he could handle them. They were fed, watered and rested, and then, if they were able to continue their journey, were sent off in the direction of their homes. Injured birds were nursed back to health, while their rings were checked. Usually Alban was able to get into contact with their owners and many were thus returned to their homes.

Alban went to work as under gardener at the Grange at the age of fourteen. He was able to make good use of his gift for making plants grow. In those days, our elders often considered that the best way to train us was to find fault with us constantly and make us aware of how unworthy we were. The head gardener was no exception. Alban had to persevere throughout continual criticism. Although he was stolid and willing, he was sensitive, too. He needed a great deal of staying power. One of his jobs, which recurred annually, was to steady the forty foot ladder used for picking the perry pears. The trees were a tremendous height. Raising the ladder to the tree was a job requiring both great strength and skill, quite apart from keeping it steady when it was in position. It was this task which fell to Alban. Mr Merriman, at the top of the ladder among the shaky branches, would expect Alban, forty feet below, to keep the ladder in place by standing on the lower rungs and 'Beearing' on it with all his strength. 'Beear on it' was a constant command shouted down to Alban, whose weight was already pressed to the ladder.

All our young people had jobs by the time they were 15 or 16 years old. Only a few had work that they really liked. The ambitious ones went to evening school to acquire skills that would help them to get better employment, while the rest found interesting hobbies which filled their leisure hours. My job with the dairy was very monotonous, but I met people and always seemed to be doing interesting things in consequence. The job had its compensations, too. For instance, we made butter each week, and in summer, before the days of refrigeration, I had to get up at 3.30am to get it finished before the day became too hot. Watching the sun swing slowly above the horizon and listening the birds as they sang their dawn chorus, were great bonuses. Getting up early paid dividends.

Although the motor car was becoming a more usual sight than it had been, in our village commercial vehicles far outnumbered cars used for leisure. One of the first privately owned motors was used partly as a hire car by its owner and the villagers enjoyed many trips through beautiful hidden Cotswold lanes and villages during the long summer evenings. Motors were expensive and money was short and we thought they would always be few and far between.

Quite suddenly we became aware that things round the village were changing. The first happening to bring this to people's attention was an advertisement in the local paper announcing that Whaddon Manor was to be sold and an auction sale of furniture and effects was soon to take place. Colonel and Mrs Jeune had been at Whaddon Manor for longer than any of the young people could remember and it seemed unthinkable that the lovely house, with its garden where Church Fetes had so often been held, and its tithe barn where we had danced so many times, should pass into other hands. It was one of the first signs of what was to happen over and over again. Colonel Jeune's heir, Hugo, had been killed in active service in 1917, and when Colonel Jeune himself died, the family decided that the heartbreaking task of selling the Manor was the only way open to them in a country where the life they had always known was fast becoming impossible.

In our complacency we thought some other family would take over the Manor and when the sale of the furniture and effects took place, most of the people from the villages of Tuffley and Whaddon were there to buy what they could afford. Many, including ourselves, bought various of the lots offered for sale, but we had an uneasy feeling that really we were looting. After that first sale, I attended many others, but could never rid myself of the feeling that I was taking part in an act of desecration. We were like a swarm of locusts which descended, took what we wanted and departed, leaving the property stripped and bare. Houses all round the district began to show the boards which gave details of forthcoming sales as more and more of them came on to the market. Auction sales became familiar events. Always they brought a chill, a sense of vandalism and increasing unease.

The people who lived in the 'big houses' in our part of England had been our leaders and benefactors and, without them, we feared for the future. Fortunately, Wynstones at Brookthorpe and the Manor at Whaddon were bought by a school, a branch of the Rudolph Steiner foundation, many of whose students became brilliant, outstanding members of their professions.

Wynstones at Brookthorpe was used as a hostel, while Whaddon Manor housed the school. I attended lectures on this system of education and found much to commend it. The Foundation is Christian based, but its religious services were held in the school itself, which meant that the churches of Brookthorpe and Whaddon both lost the support of the family in their 'big house'. The loss was serious in each case.

Our parents did their best to keep their growing young people occupied. Dad acquired a billiards table, which also had a table tennis top and for summer evenings he made two cricket bats and sets of stumps. The bats were

An aerial view of Whaddon Manor, now Wynstones School. St. Margaret's Church is screened by trees beyond.

heavy and stung our hands — when we managed to hit the ball. For the next two summers we were expected to turn out two evenings a week to join his cricket team. If it was wet, we took turns to play table tennis or billiards. 'Dad's Team' included everyone who could be persuaded to join us, plus a few friends from Gloucester.

Old Bill's garden bordered the paddock and on fine evenings he and his wife contentedly leaned on the fence watching the game — Old Bill puffing away at his clay pipe, which he removed from his mouth from time to time as he made comments on the play. If we slacked at fielding or batting, he told us about it. Of course, Father's home-made wine was part of the attraction for the men of the team.

The team folded up after my sister and brother both got settled sweethearts, though billiards and home-made wine still attracted the men.

I took to writing plays, which kind friends acted, and we provided (we hoped) entertaining evenings for village people and help for charities. Through this interest, I came to realise that I was sadly lacking in musical and dancing ability and decided to join a School of Music in Gloucester. This was more easily dreamed up than done! I wrote for an interview and subsequently met the girl who might become my teacher. Margery Deavin was already well known in music circles, as she competed with her pupils at places as far off as Bristol and Birmingham, while the Cheltenham Festival always occupied the school for its duration.

Margery was equally competent both as an artist and teacher. After a short talk, during which we recognised a mutual liking, she put a copy of Offenbach's *Barcarolle*, from his *Tales of Hoffman*, on the piano. I looked at it in the fascinated way a rabbit eyes a snake. Margery asked for the right hand only, which I was just about able to supply. Then she said, 'If you can learn this by next week, I'll take you on, otherwise I'm afraid it's no use'. Although despairing of being able to read and play the piece by the following week, I worked at it with fiendish energy and when the next lesson came I could just manage to get through it. Great relief!

My sister had always been able to sight-read the right hand, and she made up the left hand as she went, which left me, a mere plodder, a lot of work to do to catch up. Her ability however, had its snags. She had three different teachers, none of whom was able to cope with Naomi's gift. Desperately they would ask, 'Where are you?' Naomi didn't know either! She was quite happy to memorise as much as she wanted and add the rest. I knew I would have to work, and work I did, harder than I had ever done, for eight happy years of dancing, singing, playing and learning theory. Spare time became a round of practice — piano, dancing, singing — then lessons and a weekly ballroom session, concerts and exams. I loved it all. At this school, students learnt to forget themselves, working with others to achieve the common good. I believe Margery's mother was the inspiration of us all. She was a very wise person, who, while imparting and sharing knowledge, made sure we all learned and shared understanding. This was true of all the family.

Margery was a joyous person, who loved life and lived it to the full, both at work and play. Her early death at 28 was a tragedy for her family and a great loss to music in Gloucester. She had been a brilliant musician herself and developed great talent in many of her students. She demanded the best and got it. I would never make a talented musician, but I learned to understand and appreciate music, to equate myself to others and to value people for their true worth.

During the 'thirties we saved, however hard it was to do so and, as a rule, people got married only after several years of saving and planning. The girls all bought linen and household equipment to put in their bottom drawers (the lowest and biggest of a chest), where our future household needs accumulated. Before World War II, people married, as a rule, only after a fairly long courtship.

By the time people could afford to get engaged, they were well past the first heady sensation of 'being in love', and either progressed to loving each other (a very different matter, which calls for mutual giving), or they realised that they were not suited for a lifetime together and parted with much less pain for all concerned than is caused by divorce. The coming of war changed all that, of course. Men who were going to war might never return, so the young married while there was still time. People were sent away to distant places, often at short notice, and long separation, combined with being thrown into the company of young and interesting folk of the opposite sex, was responsible for the break-up of what could and should have been many a happy marriage.

Houses seemed to be just as scarce and difficult to acquire for those with little money as they are nowadays, but the waiting time was passed in making preparation for the home that was to come later. Many couples began their married lives with the parents of one side or the other, leaving when a house became vacant.

Probably the greatest benefit the passing years brought to our village was a bus of our own! Well, not quite that really, but a privately owned bus which served the villages of Brookthorpe, Whaddon and Lower and Upper Tuffley, connecting them with Gloucester.

It made three or four journeys each day, which was sufficient for the needs of most of us. The bus was owned and driven by George Beard, a happy, smiling man, who was always ready with a cheerful greeting. He soon got to know everyone and some pleasant joke always met us as we climbed up the steep steps to his driving seat and paused to pay. It would be, 'Morning, Mrs Jones, how's the rheumatism today?' as some stout body struggled aboard. If anyone was late, and George saw the running figure, he never minded keeping the bus waiting for a few minutes. It was a happy bus; everybody knew everybody else and greetings were shouted from one end of it to the other. Shafts of country wit often rocked the whole company with mirth as everyone joined in, and the talk was so vivacious that it often drowned the not inconsiderable noise of the engine.

George would park his bus near the centre of Gloucester, where it was easy for those laden with shopping bags to go and dump them before returning to the shops for further purchases. He was ready to oblige by delivering parcels for 6d a time and had been known to go to the chemist's to get a prescription made up for a patient who was too ill to do it for himself and had no one else to fetch his medicine. That bus was a jolly, rattling, rolling mine of information for all who travelled in it; news went from one end to the other during the trip and Lower Tuffley certainly enjoyed George's contribution to progress.

A village hall was built in the middle of Grange Road during the mid-'thirties. It was to become, temporarily, the church of St. George. During the week, the wooden building was used for many activities, including a Youth Club, where I helped for a time, while most of my contemporaries were getting married and leaving the village. As my musical ability developed I began to play the harmonium for the Sunday evening services and, slowly, began to grow away from St. Margaret's at Whaddon, going instead to the hall each week.

St. Margaret's had, for years, been losing the girls of its choir, as one after another got married. Then our organist, who had been with the church for many years, left to go to another which had a larger organ. I was left as the sole survivor on the girls' side, and, long before taking the step of leaving, I had felt very lonely.

As St. George's Hall was situated in the centre of the village, many more people attended the services than if they had had to go to Whaddon. This break with the past was to be the first of many for me.

At this time there was a growing feeling of apprehension in the air. In Germany Hitler had been gaining more and more power. His demands knew no bounds as he moved from the conquest of one country to another, with scarcely a pause. The German people seemed mesmerised by his personality. Even so, it was not until late one evening after a dance that the full meaning of events suddenly became clear to me.

For many years Life will continue at a certain pace, and so it had been in

Lower Tuffley between the wars. We got used to living in a set way. It might be that some, more adventurous, worked harder or with more acumen than the rest of us, becoming wealthy of famous, but most of us were quite content to make a reasonable living and enjoy the pleasure of the day until, perhaps quietly or perhaps suddenly, we came to the end of our human span. We might be poor, we had no Welfare State; the dreams which had led men to fight for their country in World War I had long dissolved, but we knew the count and lived accordingly.

The early part of the decade had been devoted to the struggle against poverty, working the land and gardens to produce as much food as possible, supplying the requirements of the family. Our soil varied, but it was good. People grew their vegetables, made their own jam and wine, kept their chickens and pigs, and gradually a feeling of increasing prosperity began to spread abroad. During the latter part of the 'thirties, the village was oppressed by an uneasy feeling of impending change.

Several factories had been built at the bottom of Tuffley Lane, offering work to women as well as men. We noted with satisfaction that Rolls Royce and Bristol Aircraft had joined forces to start a works on the other side of Gloucester, which promised to employ more and more people. We found that we could no longer keep men and women who had worked for us for years, because they could earn much more in the factories. For the first time in years there were more jobs available than there were people to fill them.

The friend who escorted me home from the dance that night was one of those who had been sent by Rolls Royce from Derby to help organise Rotol. As we talked before saying goodnight, he suddenly said something about, 'When the war comes'. I was startled. 'War won't come again!' I exclaimed, 'Mr Chamberlain has said there will be 'Peace in our time'.' 'Then why do you suppose our factory is being built?' he asked.

For the first time the vague uneasiness crystallised into understanding. I foresaw something of what must come. Suddenly I felt cold and realised that I was shaking. Our village had only just recovered from the previous holocaust. I thought, 'But another war — and worse than before!'

Life lost some of its brightness from that time on. Instead of wondering whether England would be involved, I began thinking about when the next war would begin.

I felt that I must have been very foolish. It had not occurred to me that the factories which had provided so much work for the people of our village and, indeed, of the city, were in preparation for war. Must there be a war to give us full employment?

We heard rumours of larger working establishments, which were to employ many more people. All our people were already busy.

One day, in a field bordering Tuffley Lane a small shed appeared. No one — even on the bus — knew why it had been erected there. Nothing seemed to go on around it, it wasn't large enough to house livestock. It was such a small shed to be built in the middle of a sizeable meadow.

Chapter Thirteen World War Two

For several days the small hut remained, locked and silent, in the middle of the field bordering Tuffley Lane. Then surveyors came with tapes and measuring instruments. They were absorbed and busy marking out the line of a new road. The stile was taken away and the hedge cut back to make room for a wide approach. The shed door was open all day now and a great deal of to-ing and fro-ing went on around it. Lorries arrived periodically, drove up the ramp on to the embryo road and tipped their loads where directed by the site foreman. They brought ballast, sleepers, and timber to line up the edges of the road. One morning a young man, who seemed to live in the shed, visited by all and sundry around him, left his shelter briefly to come to the edge of the lane and ask us to deliver a half pint of milk daily. He said, 'I asked at the farm, but they couldn't be bothered', then added, as an afterthought, 'By the way, we'll need more milk later on'.

For a week I left the half pint of milk as requested and at the end of that time the stores in the field included kerb stones, and posts had been erected to show where future buildings would be. Workmen came and began to level the road and lay down hard core, so that, come winter or wet weather, the lorries would be able to come and go without sinking up to their axles in the soft ground.

Some of the workmen asked for milk and sales increased. Building materials now flooded into the site and one day I asked the site foreman what all the buildings were going to be. 'Oh', he said, hardly pausing in his work, 'there will be houses'. 'How many?' I asked. 'Couldn't say', he replied briefly. In answer to an enquiry as to whether the houses would be for sale, he just said 'No'. I wondered who would live there, but there seemed to be no satisfactory answers to all the questions that came to mind. The speed of the building increased daily; trowels rang on brick and the men worked at a steady pace, 'Piece work', was the terse reply to my question. Thus began a period of secrecy which lasted for years, strange and chilling in a village where, hitherto, we had all known each other and what was going on.

As the number of men increased, so did the demand for milk and I began to have difficulty in keeping up with my regular work, delivering milk to the older houses in Tuffley Lane.

A gang of Irishmen came to lay sewers and the amount of milk they consumed was astonishing. They worked in a dogged, non-stop fashion and it gradually dawned on me that behind all this activity lay some matter of great urgency. A whole row of houses took shape; as soon as the bricklayers finished, the carpenters moved in, roof timbers were erected and the hod carriers scurried up and down ladders, carrying their loads of tiles for the roofs. Lorries continually blocked the narrow lane and on the site the surveyor and road gang had laid down two roads, one cutting through the allotments, which had, until then, been sacrosanct, and only ending at the edge of the paddock that we rented. The other road bisected the first and ended opposite Whitecombe Farm.

The year was 1939 and the summer sun shone continuously from a hot, cloudless sky. The men worked in khaki shorts and boots, having discarded their shirts. Their thirst seemed insatiable, but the foreman, intent on keeping them working, forbade the men to come down off the scaffolding to get milk, so that, if no hod carrier was at hand, I had to climb ladders and run along the boards to give it to them. Many of these men were rough and hard living individuals, but I never heard a dirty remark or any undue swearing when I did this. I always wore riding breeches and a shirt, which made climbing about easier. I appreciated their thoughtfulness.

As September approached, the second house in Tuffley Lane, at the Grange Road end, was finished. This was to be the show house, which meant that whoever lived there had to be prepared to show it to viewers, if required. The foreman wanted someone to clean the house first and an enquiry in the village soon produced a scrubber *par excellence* who was more than pleased with the remuneration she received.

I endured nightmare times at the weekends, on Saturday afternoons and Sundays, trying to collect the milk bottles. These might be left in the most inaccessible places, often thrown down between the scaffolding boards, where they landed in wet clay. Sometimes the bottles were left half full of cement or covered in plaster; a few, and these gave us the most trouble, had been used to hold paraffin. They were an awful nuisance for, while when the paraffin had dried up it lost its smell, immediately it was put into hot water the penetrating vapour spread, until it permeated the whole batch of bottles going through the baths on their way to the sterilizer. Finding the offending bottle was a difficult business and, when found, it had to be isolated and cleaned many times over separately, while the rest of the batch had to be re-washed until no smell remained. Eventually,we found it easier and more hygienic to use cartons. On one occasion, the result for me was a failed music exam, when time and temper ran out.

The speed of the building never slackened. Sundays were the quietest days, but if one section of the work was lagging behind the rest, then the Sabbath was used to catch up.

We knew that every available man and woman in the village was at work, but we did not realise that this building operation was being dovetailed to establishements being built to decentralize men and equipment from London; foresight fully justified as the war progressed and London was so badly bombed.

Although the show house had been finished and was ready for occupation, the space which was to be its garden was a dreadful sight. A lovely old orchard had been bulldozed, though a few of the perry pear trees had been left. Logs lay about on the surface of the churned up yellow clay, and drums of all sizes, together with the bricks left over from the building work, were scattered far and wide. No fences had been put up and it looked as if months of work would be needed before anyone could make this desert blossom like the rose. Yet, given time, that is just what the house's owners did. Roses bloomed everywhere and the garden was always full of vegetables. There was no sign of the yellow clay.

One September Sunday morning, a message was broadcast over the radio. It told us that Great Britain was at war with Germany. The scattered pieces of the jigsaw fell into place; the secrecy made sense at last.

Just over a fortnight later, the first occupants of the new house moved in. A gap had to be cut in the deep thorn hedge to admit their furniture. Fortunately, the weather was fine and still warm; furniture vans had a habit of sinking into the morass of clay on wet days. All vehicles slithered and skidded on the muddy surface and at times Wellington boots became so bogged down that their wearer was forced to leave them behind. Our village bus service turned into a driver's nightmare as George and his vehicle came face to face with lorries carrying loads of every kind of building material—bricks, timber, cement, window frames, etc.

From their London flat, the first family, Mr and Mrs Heard and Pat, came to settle in this chaos. Pat was then three years old. It was as I was collecting empty bottles that I saw them first—sitting on crates that had been set down in their lounge—and promptly received my first order for milk to be delivered on what came to be known locally as 'the Estate'. They said that they had come from London. They looked very cheerful and told me that the incoming people would all be Government employees.

Furniture was still being transferred from the van to the house as George's bus appeared, turning into Tuffley Lane from Grange Road, and George was faced with the enormous bulk of the removal van, which took up most of the road. George put his elbow on the steering wheel and leant his face on his hand as he considered the possibilities. If the van were to move a little nearer to the house, one side would be in a shallow ditch and George might just be able to squeeze past.

The passengers fell silent and viewed the newcomers speculatively. It was most unusual for the bus to be silent, but everyone in it felt a shock as they realised that the village where we had all lived for so many years was in the process of disappearing—vanishing under new roads and rows of red brick houses. Were not the first occupants actually moving in?

After a great deal of backing up and pulling in, the bus eventually got past the furniture van and a sigh of relief went from one end to the other. Talk was resumed and, by the time the travellers reached the Stroud road, the bus was its noisy old self again.

It was difficult to imagine how people who had been used to living comfortably in a busy city would be able to adapt to the dreadful conditions in which they now found themselves—this wilderness that the builders had created in our village—but settle they did, quickly and energetically. The builders cleared away most of their debris and a man was found to rough-dig the gardens after fences (two rows of wire stretched between posts) had been put up.

These people were surrounded by problems but tradesmen constituted the worst of them. With the outbreak of war, supplies began to run short and no one wanted to take on extra customers. From the baker to the coalman, none could feel sure of getting his quota of goods. Rationing and the children's special milk allowance added to the dificulties of our particular business, but we managed to get enough eggs, butter and milk (supplemented by the tinned variety) to go round.

As our friends were the first people to move in, they took on the onerous job of helping the next to come with their problems and I was liable at any time to be faced with the difficulty of finding some house where a family could store their furniture for a few days — or weeks — while their own house was being completed.

Families moved in at the rate of about two each week to begin with, but this soon accelerated until four or five houses would be occupied in as many days. We constantly badgered our farmer either to buy more cows or somehow, by some means, produce more milk and life became something of a nightmare. We used to get up at five o'clock in the morning and often fell over the builders' rubble in the pitch darkness as we made our rounds. Somehow we managed to take it all in our stride, though I must confess that tripping over a dog's chain stretched across a path, or falling into an icy puddle, were never my idea of entertaining fun.

Although the blitzes and the long night watches during air raids were still months away, our village had already been blitzed by the builders as surely as if a battle had been fought over its fields. The invading bricks and mortar had already devoured an oblong stretch of between a quarter and half a mile, and there was no hint of the pace slackening. We added two roads of houses and one side of Tuffley Lane to our morning round, as well as supplying the builders, and life was tough.

Once more our young men disappeared into the forces and our girls into various war jobs and the older generation was left to carry on at home. A feeling of prosperity was everywhere as people settled into their new homes, got their blackout curtains up and their houses straight, and then the men were off on their bicycles or in loaded cars to their work in the factories or depots, which seemed to have sprung up everywhere. An estate of factories at the bottom of Lower Tuffley Lane absorbed many. But although the population was increasing week by week, there were still no shops. People had come from places where all the conveniences of modern life were on the doorstep, found it a considerable hardship to have to walk two miles and more into the city and then, after shopping, having to make the same journey back on foot, weighed down by laden baskets. Finding help, whether for our house or business, became more and more difficult. But still the houses continued to be built. The other side of Tuffley Lane was eaten up and Podsmead became a network of roads. It seemed as if some insatiable monster was consuming our village, field by field, orchard by orchard. There was any amount of felled wood, but few had the heart or energy to go wooding. For, in spite of all the trade and all the wages the building brought, there was little time for light-hearted banter now.

Just occasionally we laughed as we had done in the earlier days—which seemed so long ago. Once, when my brother was on leave, he decided he needed some exercise, and, climbing a tree that was about to be felled, he sawed away at one of the branches. Unfortunately for him, he was sitting on the end furthest away from the tree trunk and was sawing the bough through between himself and the tree. My friend, Simmy, and I watched him from her window, wondering how long he could continue sawing before the limb broke away. This happened at last and he went crashing down with the tree branch into a muddy wet ditch below. We knew he was not hurt and the resulting laugh brought relief.

George's bus was soon quite inadequate for the number of people who wished to go shopping and many would-be passengers had to walk into the town. The bus was no longer a merry place where one met one's friends for a gossip, but a necessity, which, like every other one, was being stretched beyond its capacity.

Strict rationing of foodstuffs was imposed by the Government and, while it provided a much fairer system than the early bird, free-for-all of the First War, it added to the worries of business people, who had to do their endless booking in the evenings.

People sent to Gloucester often arrived at what had once been a peaceful village late on a dark winter night. They had little or no chance of viewing their houses before moving in; the speed with which the occupants arrived never slackened. Those who came first, tackled and solved newcomers problems for which they had come all unprepared. House cleaners and people to rough-dig the gardens were found for them; food for those who had looked to Tuffley as an area where necessities could be purchased; rabbits or chickens from the farm for those who had no meat—the problems were endless. All this brought an atmosphere of great kindness and fellow feeling in everyone. Each helped the other without waiting to be asked and step by step we acquired that great camaraderie which was to endure throughout the war. Those of us who experienced it look back in happy remembrance.

The country was prepared now. Whatever Neville Chamberlain had, or had not, achieved with his scrap of paper, he had gained six months and more of time for England to square up and prepare for what everyone knew must be a life and death struggle. When Winston Churchill assumed command, the lion, which had lain couchant for twenty-one years, became rampant and started to roar.

As more and more houses were finished and their occupants arrived, the village became inundated with newcomers. George's bus now, quite definitely, was unable to cope with the growing numbers and at the bus stops there were frequently heated discussions. Petitions and begging letters were sent to the Corporation and, in time, George and his lovely bus were driven off the roads as the City responded by sending their vehicles out to meet the growing need. Now we knew no more than half the people with whom we travelled and conversations concerned merely common problems and the weather.

Tuffley Lane was the last road to be made up and one awful winter the ruts of snow and ice froze six to nine inches deep, which made the task of pushing the laden bicycle combination along almost impossible. Even the van was difficult to manipulate. We and our helpers were delivering a hundred gallons of milk before breakfast each day. Somehow we coped but my precious music had to be sacrificed, as did most other people's hobbies. Time—free time—was very short indeed.

At first the local people did not know what to make of the newcomers, but one thing was certain, they had tremendous courage. They moved their furniture into their houses, hung up their blackout curtains and, as soon as their concrete paths were laid and dry, they began to tackle the waste land which surrounded them. Many had never possessed gardens previously and though those who are still alive look back, laughing, at their early mistakes, they learned quickly and well.

Their houses became shining examples to the rest of us for the most part and slowly gardens emerged, filled with vegetables and flowers. The heavy clay was tamed and the soil improved, though it is still difficult to cultivate in either dry or very wet weather. We all laughed about the early mishaps and mistakes. There was the lady who cut and cooked a whole row of promising cauliflower plants which her husband had recently planted, because she thought they would make a nice green vegetable, not realising they would have grown big if they had been allowed to develop. They would have made at least twenty meals when fully grown.

Another, doing her best to liven up a dull time, picked all the kidney bean flowers to use as table decorations, to cheer her husband up. He was a sport and enjoyed the sight of them, which was just as well since there would be no beans to follow for some time. At first, people used to cut their beans with scissors instead of picking them.

The Severn Bore was an unknown phenomenon to the newcomers, who were also unused to seeing every spring morning dull and drizzly until such time as the tide had receded. Mr friend Simmy was greatly mystified when, as I delivered a load of flower roots for her garden one morning, I remarked that they should grow well because it was Bore weather. She pondered on it for some time before asking what was meant by Bore weather. It is a fact that the cloudiness and fine rain combined with warmth each day does seem to help growth and produce fine crops.

Hardly had our new neighbours moved in before evacuees were brought in to the village from Birmingham. They were frightened, tough, city children and they kept their foster parents continually busy. One friend who worked with us told me that her two evacuees had never been in a large bath and screamed with fright the first time they were bathed.

Whaddon School became too overcrowded and could not take any more children, so another, temporary school was erected near Grange Road. This was to be the first of many new schools.

When we got used to all the upheavals, we began to enjoy life once again and, although times had changed forever for all of us, there were great compensations. Those of us who were fit and free enough, trained for wartime jobs in the evenings. Some became Air Raid Wardens, others First Aiders, while the members of our football team, who were either unfit for service or already doing war work, joined the Home Guard. We all had a whale of a time, bandaging people who did not want to be bandaged, worrying each other to death over chinks of light left showing and as for the Home Guard! — We all enjoyed a Dad's Army of our very own a long time before television thought of it.

As a football team they had been one of the village's more energetic assets. Mr Percy Andrews, father of Lilian (a friend since our schooldays), who had shared all the things which we village children had been lucky enough to experience such as the Choir, the School, Guides, outings, had been trainer of the team for so long that they made him a life member. The family garage, which was quite large, was the changing room for the team, who also used the huge bath in the wash-house at the rear. Their trainer stoked up a large boiler there, until the water was piping hot. Four men could get into the bath at one time and, without any 'by your leave' or 'do you mind?' Percy would throw buckets full of hot water over them. Lilian told me that, at times, their screams used to ring through the house! Mr Andrews also acted as First Aid man to the team and, after a match, he would bring the injured ones to his home and rubbed in so much embrocation that the whole house reeked of it.

The Home Guard trained in the evenings and at weekends at Matson and locally, of course, under Colonel Sinnott. Training was hard work and caused mighty thirsts which needed slaking. Our intrepid Dad's Army often finished their stint by marching to the New Inn. One night, their thirst was so bad that, when they had quenched it, the men made their way back to the village, only to find when they arrived at Grange Road, that they had left their weapons behind them in the New Inn!

On another occasion, Percy and his son-in-law were homeward bound from the New Inn after their evening's stint, when anti-aircraft guns began firing. Sewers were being laid in Tuffley lane at the time, and Percy made a beeline for the nearest pipe at great speed, shouting to his son-in-law, 'Come in here, you silly b...' Ken, who was in the Air Force and home on leave, stood and laughed at our intrepid Home Guard.

In the early days of the war, we all (Wardens, Home Guard and First Aiders) used to meet halfway along Grange Road and wait there in case there was an air raid. As soon as the sirens sounded, some ducks, belonging to Sam Crowther, a member of the Home Guard, would start quacking. Indeed, some people swore that they did not wait for the warning but heard the sound of the approaching German planes before we received notification! As meat was scarce, the rest of the men used to tease Sam, saying that they would shoot and eat the birds before they could give away the village's position. Sam pretended to get very concerned, but, needless to say, the ducks were never shot.

We got to know the sound of the enemy bombers as they passed overhead; the 'woom-woom' of their engines was easy to distinguish from the even rhythm of our own machines. As a rule, the enemy bombers passed over Gloucester on their way to bomb Birmingham or Coventry, and we could see the awful glare of the fires left burning from our village. Some nights Gloucester was ringed with fire from Cardiff, Bristol, Birmingham and Coventry. We knew our greatest danger came from returning aircraft, which would dump their loads of undropped bombs anywhere, just to lighten a crippled plane. The mist which spread over the valley at nights from the Severn gave our village and the city a large measure of safety.

There were some hilarious times when all our Civil Defence Forces were out practising at the same time. The Home Guard and the Air Raid Wardens gave counter orders and we all fought each other to be the ones to attend 'casualties'. Some of our worthy citizens objected strongly when they were informed they were casualties and must be bandaged and carted off on stretchers. It was all very inconvenient. We laughed over it, knowing how tragic things might become.

A square of soil was excavated in the orchard at home, supposedly for an air raid shelter, but as it was in the path of the spring which fed our well, it quickly filled with water, so that we had the option of either staying indoors and waiting to be bombed or drowning in the air raid shelter!

One source of fun the war did not take from us was the joy of producing our own pantomimes and in this the people from London soon proved their worth. They asked to join in and gave great assistance, from Ruth Allen, who had

The happy cast of 'Cinderella'.

been a wardrobe mistress at Drury Lane theatre, to Simmy, who played the piano on sight. The menfolk helped as well and our wartime Cinderella was the best pantomime we had ever put on. We were fortunate because rehearsals rarely coincided with air raid warnings and the dancing practice I had put in proved of great value.

Our Company was about thirty strong and we practised long and hard all through the summer months, ready for the winter. With materials rationed, dressing the cast was a real headache but luckily such stuffs as butter muslin, sateen, and curtain nets and fabrics, were unrationed. The only coupons we needed were for Prince Charming's outfit and he (she, of course) had a costume of white satin, with a beautiful lace jabot, and ruffles at the cuffs. Lace was still obtainable then.

The butter muslin we made into tutus. These had to be stiffened and, as we were unable to get starch (shortages cropped up in all sorts of peculiar places), Lilian and other members of the Company spent hours dipping skirts into flour and water, drying them and then ironing them. These bouffant skirts were draped all round Lilian's kitchen as she tirelessly ironed one after another of the small fairies' dresses.

The Andrews' garage was our practice room, so that no one needed to go very far from home, which was an important consideration in those uncertain days. The pantos helped to give us all a boost, though finding time for practice was difficult.

Pantomimes always seemed to have a certain effect on some of the married players. We had only to put the play out for reading and then, for sure, one of the performers would become pregnant. Lilian learned that she would soon have an addition to her family during a panto which we put on before the war began. We let out her clothes repeatedly and she continued with the production until the end of performances. I saw her one evening a little later and asked her how she felt. She said, 'The baby is late. I'd love to go for a walk'. I offered to go with her and we completed a short, sedate stroll. Arriving back at her home, Lilian said, 'I'd like to do it again', so we repeated the walk. Leaving her apparently all right, I headed for home. Later she told me that I had only been gone a few minutes when the baby decided it was time to be born. Her brother went off to Gloucester on his bicycle to fetch the Nurse, but the baby was not going to wait for any nurse. Realising the urgency, someone said, 'Fetch Granny Hayward'. Mrs Hayward came at the trot. When she arrived, she said to Lilian, 'We'll get this baby before Nurse comes'. They did, and when the nurse got there, she was presented with the newly-born, lovely, baby girl, already washed, dressed and wrapped in her shawl. The poor nurse's face fell. That baby was to have been her last before she finished her training and became a fully fledged District Nurse. In the event, she had to wait another nine months before delivering her final baby.

When our wartime production of Cinderella began, Lilian's outfit as Prince Charming was considered to be one of the most important and Ruth Allen made it beautifully. Sometime later, Lilian tried on the breeches and jacket and found it rather tight. Ruth let it out. But again when she tried it on, Lilian found it too close a fit, and Ruth got rather impatient. She said she could not keep letting it out and asked her to try eating less. The trousers had to be tied together at the top eventually, and Lilian continued until the end of the run. As we closed our production, she told us she was once again four months pregnant. Simmy found that she was in the same condition and later on produced a lovely baby boy, who became my first godson.

Travel during the war became something of a nightmare. Petrol, rationed of course, was in very short supply, and many people put bricks under the chassis of their cars, so that the tyres were off the ground, and left their vehicles to their fate for the duration. Bus services, which really needed to expand, were everywhere curtailed, causing long queues and short tempers. Even when the long-awaited bus did arrive, more often than not it would be almost full and the people at the end of the queue had to go on waiting at the stop for the next one. Often there were hourly intervals between buses. Sometimes conductors' 'stood by their rights' and only took on sitting passengers, turning off those who were standing in the aisle, and an even longer queue than usual was the result. If the bus happened to be the last one, hitching a lift was the only alternative to a long walk home.

My fiancé and I were faced with this situation when, on a rare day off, we had travelled to Newnham-on-Severn. The sun shone down warmly; it was refreshing to be away from the atmosphere of war by which we were constantly surrounded. We explored the church, the river bank and walked in the country. About five o'clock, we joined the bus queue just as the bus arrived at the stop. We were part of the tail end which was left behind and the usual hour's wait faced us all. Finally, after the long wait, the last bus of the day came along. Suddenly, from somewhere nearby, two people, who certainly had not been in the queue, appeared and boarded the bus ahead of all the rest of us. Despite the heated argument which broke out, they were allowed to stay. One by one, the conductor counted the passengers as they climbed aboard and, behind the couple standing just in front of us, his arm came across the door and he flatly refused to allow anyone else on the bus. It was one of the days when he, too, was 'standing up for his rights'. In vain we pleaded that we had been there for the previous bus, while the two people who got on first were the last to arrive. Whether those two were acquaintances of his, we did not know, but he settled the argument by pushing the bell button and the bus leapt away, disappearing into the dusty distance. There were several others besides us left at the stop, including an elderly man. We had just decided that we would have to walk the ten miles back to Gloucester when a lorry, carrying an obviously heavy, flat-topped load, slowed and stopped by the queue. 'Want a lift?' shouted the driver. Thanking him, we lost no time in all climbing up to the top of his load. We helped 'Grandad' on first. He was rather stiff but very willing to be heaved up. Perched on top of the flat-topped load, we all felt very grateful. The seat was hard, but who cared? We trundled on until the lorry reached the City outskirts when what should we see but the bus which had so callously left us to our fate! Obviously, it had been stationary for some time. The passengers stood about looking dejected. We all waved gaily and then noted with (I am sorry to say) satisfaction that one of the bus's tyres was flat. Grandad chuckled and the rest of us broke into cheers and loud laughter.

As we reached Westgate bridge, the driver stopped the lorry and said, 'Sorry, I can't take you any further'. We didn't mind, we were thankful to have come so far. The driver refused to take any payment, 'No, no, my pleasure', he said.

As we prepared to go our separate ways home he asked, 'Do you want to know what you were riding on?'

We waited expectantly.

'Dynamite', he said briefly.

We laughed with him as we waved 'Goodbye'.

Chapter Fourteen   Shamus

Shamus was a golden retriever, gentle, shy, yet always possessing an appearance of nobility. His coat shone and waved and curled, his tail and leg feathers were soft as silk. His head and shoulders were reminiscent of the larger St. Bernard. He had beautiful flecked amber eyes and his expression changed a hundred times a day. His name was shortened to Sham.

Sham was a war casualty. When his home in Exeter was bombed, he was trapped in the rubble and although he sustained no physical injuries, the experience left him ill with shell shock. His first owners brought him with them to Gloucester, where there was work for his master and a house for him and his wife. Unfortunately, the house had only a small garden and after his unnerving experience, Sham would not go into any house. At first, for many months, he shook all over with terror when any roof enclosed him.

His owners met our father and told him about the dog, knowing we had room for him to run loose. Dad tried to persuade me to adopt Sham, but the war had brought heavy responsibilities and I had enough to do without taking on the burden of an animal so ill and who would be in need of so much love and care.

Sham's master and mistress clinched the matter by bringing him to our house and leaving him. They must have been heartbroken in doing this, but the alternative was that he would have to be destroyed.

I loved him at once, but saw the difficulties which lay ahead and feared for him and myself. His master and mistress said he had previously always lived outside, so he had a bed in one of our large sheds. He must have felt utterly deserted and alone, because we had to keep the shed door closed in case he ran away. He was grieving a lot for them and for a long time he did not recognise me as his nearest companion. When we went out, I was obliged to keep him on a lead in case he ran away. I hated the thought of his loneliness and unhappiness and tried to make him happier by giving him extra grooming and visiting him as often as possible. His great wistful eyes haunted me, I tried to show him I loved him and hoped he understood, but every time we went out, he tried to follow the trail of his late owners and wanted to get away.

His food was my greatest worry. He took only very little and only if I fed him.

One night, when our Company was rehearsing for a pantomime, news was brought to me that Shamus had run away. We stopped rehearsal and turned ourselves into a search party, fifty strong. We split into twos and scoured miles of lanes and fields and part of Gloucester for three hours—in vain. As the darkness fell on a velvet autumn evening, our members returned wearily home. Their great kindness and sympathy were typical of the people in our village. Our local people had always given help in time of need and our new neighbours seemed to be just as kindhearted to us all.

I felt sick at heart, for in the few days I had known Shamus, I had learnt to love him; to lose him at this time would have been dreadful. Then just as some friends and I turned into the orchard, we heard his deep, low woof. He had returned of his own accord. He bounded straight up to me and demonstrated his joy by jumping up and putting his paws on my shoulders, a thing he only rarely did. My relief was near to pain. After saying our thanks and good nights to our friends, I calmed Shamus and fed him before putting him to bed.

The next morning, Shamus was very ill. He lay almost cold and could only just raise his head and lift the end of his tail in a wag. We dressed him in one of my father's old woollen vests and covered him with straw to warm him. For some days he took only a little egg and milk from a bottle, but gradually he improved. Our mother was a great help at this time. She was always a good nurse to children and animals alike, and though she had steadfastly refused to have anything to do with Sham previously, she now helped me tremendously with her great experience. Together we watched over him until at last he began to improve.

As he recovered, I lost my fear that Sham would leave me, he seemed to have accepted us all and I was able to let him loose on the short walks which were all his strained heart could now manage. Our friendship grew and we were able to trust each other more and more, and steadily he became stronger.

Shamus never lost his fear of air raids and used to sit and shiver from the time the warning sirens sounded until the 'all clear' was heard. I went to him whenever my work allowed. He would never enter the house at these times, though at ordinary times he began to venture inside for short periods before sitting and begging to be taken out again. He hated confined spaces.

When he was unsure or afraid, he always came to me; we understood each other so well that each knew what the other thought. If any other member of the family gave Sham an order, he always turned to me to see what I thought about it, and unless I endorsed it he refused to obey. Always he was gentle and loving and his dependence made me feel very responsible for him.

How I wished I had known him as a blundering puppy, when his family chose him because, ears flapping, he had rushed to meet them ahead of his brothers and sisters and all the other pups in the Kennels where he was reared.

He must have been so soft and mischievous, and so beautiful. He was always mischievous, he chewed countless numbers of my belongings, chiefly I think because they belonged to me and the scent was familiar to him. Summer holidays with his first family had included many visits to the seaside, where his days were spent in one long round of swimming, then digging a huge hole in the sand and finally lying in the hole and falling asleep until it was time to dig the next hole and take another bathe.

He must have been a delightful companion in those days. He was always a joy to watch, the sun burnished his coat with living fire, and when he was well he seemed full of the zest for living.

Many of our happiest hours were spent in the fields during that time. In those fields, in the misty early mornings when the spring was very young, Shamus chased imaginary rabbits or real partridges (I nearly stepped on a nest of newly hatched young birds one day. They are so wonderfully camouflaged that it is difficult to see them. The parents always run off screaming to draw off people's attention and try to induce intruders to alter course). He never attempted to touch one, but his nature was to retrieve and he was always excited when he scented game. While he galloped along, ears blown back, searching the wind for scent of rabbit or other game, I hunted the hedges for violets and bluebells.

These morning and evening walks were pure magic to me, the scent of pear blossom covering the old tall trees like white snow or apple blossom shading from palest pink to deep rose in the cider apple orchard, I shall never forget, even though I will never see them again; for there are no orchards left in Lower Tuffley now; they have given place to row upon row of red brick houses as far as the eye can see. In those days, the deep tender blue of the sky shone through the latticed branches. The sky is still beautiful and the air clean, but the wild roses, with their deep pink petals and haunting fragrance, have disappeared, along with the fields of wheat splashed with the blood red of the poppies, and tall mowing grass, rippling like a green sea before a light summer breeze, where later Shamus stumbled over the thick lays of hay and snorted under them as his wishful thinking turned to rabbits.

In June there would be a huge patch of purple vetch on a railway embankment, which I have never seen anywhere else; I used to go and sit there with Sham and together we would watch the huge GWR steam engines as they chuffed and strained to pull their heavy loads up a steady incline, the steepest part of their journey from Gloucester to London.

Autumn brought berries, tawny and black, with leaves shading from palest yellow to russet. The warm scents of evening mingled with bonfire smoke, there were blackberries to be picked, and mushrooms. All these things had gone from Lower Tuffley. There are no longer any fields or orchards and the steam trains have given way to oil-fired engines.

Always then Sham was busy with quests of his own, which often ended in some hedge. In the snow the tracks of animals were easy for me to follow, but Sham needed the scent of things and snow killed it. He was bothered about having to proceed using his eyes alone, he found tracking much more difficult without scent. Occasionally we struck the single line trail of the fox and followed it as far as we were able.

Once, when he was alone, the dog found a nest of baby rabbits and brought them home so gently, one by one. Poor little things they were nearly always dead from fright when he arrived with them. He was so gentle, he would never have killed one deliberately.

Sham never ran in a straight line, but ambled along with a sideways movement, which caused us great amusement. He also hated negotiating stiles and many a time, when no nearby gap was available, I had to lift him — both of us grunting — over the top. His head pointed in the direction he wanted to go, while his forelegs always seemed to want to get to the right hand side of the road before the end of the journey. Funnily enough, he always finished up where he wanted to go.

Following the course of Sandfords brook, also known as Daniels brook, which marks the boundary between Lower Tuffley and Quedgeley, he chased water rats which he never caught, and on one glorious occasion he found an otter which eluded him easily, slipping down into the deep darkness of a pool and swimming under water. He got very excited over the chase and it did not seem to matter that he caught nothing. The brook was a succession of deep pools, where eels lived, and shallow crystal-clear water, peopled with minnows, flashing silver as the sunlight caught them in a thousand points of light. These were watched by the kingfishers working to feed their hungry brood hidden in the steep banks of the brook. The parents flashed down on to their prey and took the small fish without breaking their flight.

The brook was lined in places with wild garlic; it gave off an unforgettable rank smell as Sham trampled it underfoot.

There was so much peace in his company. England was then engaged in deadly warfare and often as we walked I watched the bombers rise heavily from a nearby aerodrome on their way to spread death and destruction on soldiers and civilians alike, or listened as air-raid sirens warned us that the enemy bombers were on their way to England to lay waste our big cities, and yet with Sham and my thoughts I felt far away from death and destruction, perhaps one valued the dear things and places more because of the knowledge of potential danger.

The encircling arm of the Cotswolds held our valley in its shelter. How true are the words of the psalmist, 'I will lift up mine eyes unto the hills, from whence cometh my help'. Those everlasting hills clothed in dark woods, whose gentle folds cast shadows as dark as purple grapes in summer, spread peace among us in spite of our knowledge of war. I sat and looked at them many, many times and, even though I have been far away from them for many years, I still remember every line of them.

At home Sham had his favourite occupations. He played for hours with a large pet rabbit, chasing it round and round and then flopping to the ground while the rabbit ran round and round him and jumped over his back, finally lying down beside the dog when he was tired.

The hen houses were raised above the ground, so that the hens had dust baths under each one. Sham thought these spaces had been left just for him, and he often disappeared while he was in the orchard. Later we would hear dull thuds as lumps of dry earth hit the floor of the fowlhouse above his head. At first the hens were terrified and any birds inside came flapping and screaming outside at a great rate. They soon got used to Sham and his hobbies and carried on with their egg laying as if he weren't there. When he was tired, he finally flopped down and went to sleep in the hole he had dug.

He loved the warmth of the fire and he loved the snow; he found joy in almost everything around him. He was very vain and enjoyed being brushed chiefly so that he might show off afterwards. He always held one of his brushes in his mouth while he was being brushed and afterwards paraded up and down before anyone who would spare time to look at him and admire him, and truly he was admirable. His wavy coat shone and rippled; he held his head proudly, and gently waved his feathery tail.

He loved to be the companion of the family's babies and was constantly with them when they visited us. We had to keep toys for him just like those they had or else he insisted on carrying one of the toys belonging to the children. At such times, lying beside the children, his melting amber eyes would half close in ecstasy, while the children delightedly pulled and pushed him. We had to restrain them at times, because he would never have complained.

Sham had one dangerous habit. He regarded motor cars as his friends and walked to meet them. His first family had always let the dog meet his master on his return from business and he was let into the car and took possession of the rear seat. This led to complications. For long after he came to us, he always ran out to meet any blue car he saw, and twice was knocked slightly. Then at his previous home there had only been his master and mistress, and Sham had always had the rear seat to himself. We were a larger family, and he had to share. How he hated it! He had a very clear way of edging behind the person next to him and eventually pushing him or her off the seat. This state of affairs could not last long, and when he eventually realised that he was only allowed half the seat, he would show his disgust by turning his back on us and sending us to Coventry. Car rides usually led to hills, where the rabbit holes were always more exciting than those he knew and visited most days.

One of the things one always had to watch for if he was in a field of cows was that he kept away from them. He was so gentle himself that he was sublimely unaware that any living thing would wish him harm. He would wander carelessly close to a cow with her calf and turn and lick the calf as if its mother did not exist. The cow, of course, terrified for her offspring, turned on him in a fury. I was always able to run fast when I was young, and many times I had to rescue him from under the horns of an irate mother.

His gentle trust of other animals made him unable to realise that all other creatures were not like him. He once became embroiled in a fight as a result. A fox terrier snarled at him repeatedly and finally bit him. Never have I seen such a change in an animal. Sham became a fury and the impudent terrier was instantly bowled over and pinned to the ground by his heavy forefeet. He did not attempt to bite the dog, but held it underfoot until I forced him to let it go.

On one occasion an evening walk filled me with terror. We had started late and darkness was falling. There had been a great deal of talk about Commandos and men were being trained to invade Germany. Doubtless the Germans were under the same sort of training in reverse. The lane down which we were walking was bordered by tall hedges, which cast dense shadows. The dog had been a little ahead of me, but returned and began walking round me in circles, his hackles raised. A horrible feeling that we were not alone took possession of me, though I could neither see nor hear anyone. The only sound was of my own footsteps. One can have an instinctive awareness of the presence of another human being, even when nothing can be discerned. Sham made no sound, but continued walking round and round me as we continued on our usual way.

Peering into a hedge, I suddenly saw a man crouching down. We continued our walk. Five yards further on another form lay in the hedge, and then another and another. There was no sound but my footsteps and we still kept moving. After about two hundred yards of this, we reached the railway arch. My mind was in a turmoil. Were these men preparing to wreck the bridge? Were the soldiers Germans or ours? It was too dark to tell. Then the dog gave a low growl. Under the bridge was an officer. He spoke to the dog quietly in perfect English, 'Be quiet, boy'. I, too, spoke to Sham and he relapsed into silence. I knew the voice to be English and could only hope the soldiers were ours. We went on some distance and then turned and began the homeward journey. There wasn't a sign of a soldier left when we reached the bridge again. I hoped it was only our men on manoeuvres.

Soon afterwards I became ill and eventually had to give up the heavy work I was doing. My father could not continue for long without my help; he had other helpers, but I had provided thinking power as well as physical strength. Dad was forced to sell our business and house and surrounding ground and he and mother retired. They took a small cottage, which again had a large garden and fields, at Eastington.

The people taking over needed to come into the house for a while to learn the business and, as things were rather difficult, I left home and went into a hostel. This broke my heart, for I had loved my home and my dog, and parting with them left me quite without support. The dog had come to love my family, but I know he missed me as I did him. The incoming people also had a dog, a fox terrier, who hated Sham, so for those few remaining weeks his life must again have been utterly miserable. The new dog tried to fight whenever he could and it was a great relief to us all when our family were able to move. Sham had gained confidence in my mother and father and, having space, he soon became happy again. I saw them all from time to time and each time it was terribly hard to leave them all. Sham always knew when I was going and sat by my belongings as long as possible.

In the new home, as in his old one, Sham found jobs for himself and performed them faithfully day by day. One of these jobs was to fetch the evening paper from the house at the top of the road. He was watched as he crossed the road and went straight to the house. As soon as he was given the paper, he would return at once, again being watched as he crossed the busy road. In the mornings, the paper was left in the gate, and as soon as Sham was let out, he would lope down the path and bring back the paper.

Another thing he loved to do was to meet the bus which brought my sister and her little boy twice each week. Sham always knew when the day was Tuesday or Thursday, and a few minutes before the bus was due, he would ask to be let out, dash to the gate and stand watching until the bus came. Then he was let out and dashed up the road to meet the two. My sister always gave him her basket to carry and he would bring it straight home with his head in the air, the little boy hanging on to his collar, his fat legs twinkling as he ran to keep pace with the dog.

The children were old enough to walk with him now and they made a lovely picture as they went far over the orchard with the great dog, all of them completely oblivious of grown-ups and utterly contented. Once, in the late spring, they all stood together under one of the tall cider pear trees, while the snowy petals planed down on them like white confetti. How many memories gathered round one dog!

During this time, I met and became engaged to my husband. Sham seemed to understand perfectly that my allegiance could not belong to him alone and a firm understanding grew up between the two of them. We took him with us for long walks on the banks of a derelict canal, home of a colony of swans, who resented our intrusion on their preserves and showed it by sticking out their long necks and hissing valedictions on us. Sham always gave them a wide berth.

When we were married, it was necessary for us to move from Gloucester to Brighton. The war ended and it was a way of life to which people had become accustomed, so that its end must mean readjustment for almost everyone. My husband was a bookseller, and his old job called. Also, his sister, who lived with his mother, married an Australian, and we felt that when she left England we should try to fill in for her. So we saw much less of them all and Sham. Heaven is not for ever in this world and one treasures the best of what has been.

Sham always chased stray cats, though he knew that our own were part of the family. He loved the kittens and when they were very young he carried them around in his mouth. They slept between his paws and, as they grew older, he and they had rough and noisy games as they chased up and down the stairs and slid all over the bedroom on the rugs. There was quite a lot of straightening up to do after them.

He loved to carry eggs he found in the orchard and this habit caused him the only walloping he ever had during our seven years together. He never broke the eggs, but always gave them to us intact. Dad had let some broody hens sit on eggs in the orchard, rather than use the incubator for just a few chickens. Although the nest boxes were securely buttoned, Sham was so intelligent that he could open them. He did this all in one day, and, putting his nose gently under the hen, he was able to take the eggs. We tried to stop him many times and in the end had to slap him. He never did it again, but it hurt us as much as it did him.

One of the funniest and almost the last memory I have of Sham was his fondness for a Pekingese belonging to my sister. This ball of fluff would run along underneath him (it must have been an instinct which came through the centuries. Pekes were used in China hundreds of years ago for hunting buffalo, and they concealed themselves in this way). We could not see the Peke until they both arrived breathless at the cottage and he emerged. They both seemed to grin at the joke.

Shamus came into my life through tragedy, and thus he went. Mother had to have a serious operation, which became much more complicated than had been expected. For days and nights we were at her bedside in a hospital ten miles distant from the cottage, and there were many hours when Shamus was alone. He knew there was great trouble and wandered from room to room and, although neighbours looked in to him, he could not settle. One morning, my father returned and found the poor dog had become frantic and in his misery had torn down curtains and bitten a hole almost through the door. He was suffering himself from tumours and we were helpless for the time. My father and brother took him to the vet before any of us saw him. We would not have been able to be with him at this time. He found peace at last.

I shall never forget going home some days later. I dreamed of Shamus for years, and felt his soft head as I stroked it in my dream. We were all so fortunate to have known him.

Chapter Fifteen   Return Journey

One should never go back, of course, yet when my husband and I had the chance of a few days' holiday that is exactly what we did.

So many things in my mind were still unresolved. What was Tuffley like after nearly forty years? Were the churches at Brookthorpe and Whaddon still as I remembered them? The Green, was it as it used to be?

We stayed at Brookthorpe and the few days spent in and around the old village were among the happiest I have ever experienced.

The first visit was to Brookthorpe church. St. Swithuns was well kept, clean and polished, with flowers beautifully arranged. We read the list of vicars who had served the church, touched the pews where the sun shone down on to them through the deeply set windows. In the porch we read again the chronogram scratched into an oak beam, which told of the death of Charles I. Someone must have ridden from London to inform the people of Brookthorpe that the King was dead—beheaded. Was he a friend or enemy of Charles? Were the people sorrowful or glad that so controversial a figure was no longer alive? No one will ever be sure. Colonel Atkyns, banished to Sapperton, must have grieved.

We looked round the old churchyard and I sat in the calm, warm peace while my husband sketched the carvings on some of the tombstones. Then we could not resist travelling to St. Margaret's church at Whaddon. We would not go into the church that day, for on the morrow an old friend would be with us and we would share the experience together. Nowadays, both the churches are kept locked, but we knew Mrs Vowles would let us in when we wished.

The summer had been wet and rather cold, but for our few days the sun shone almost continuously. The farmers were busy with their bumper harvests; the Dutch barns stacked to their roofs with bales of hay, the men and machines coping with the ripened corn. The countryside was filled with a great peace.

We spoke briefly to Mrs Vowles and then walked slowly along the winding path to the church door and looked into the porch. The framed list of men from Tuffley, Whaddon and Brookthorpe, who had served and died during World War I, was still there. Such a long list from three small villages. Following the contour of the church, we looked at the gravestones as we went. The churchyard was still kept beautifully neat and tidy. More of the old friends of my childhood had joined those whose last resting place was so well known to me. Eliza Long Knapp's memorial was still as it used to be.

Among the newer graves was the stone set up for Ethel and Ernest Haines and I paused to remember them. Such beautiful names are to be found on these memorials to the past: Comfort, Adela, Quinella.

My husband was drawing again, taking details of tablets let into the wall of the church. I wandered, content, touching the warm stones, reading the inscriptions where they had not been defaced by time and weather. The sun, low in the sky, still filled the peaceful place. I looked once more on Muriel's little headstone, but the inscription was too weather-worn to read. On the red granite stone set in remembrance of the Lee Williams family are words from Tennyson's *Crossing the Bar* — 'Twilight and evening bell, And after that the dark'. I suddenly felt, most surely **not** 'After that the dark'. After that, rather, light and warmth!

Evening advanced and we returned to Brookthorpe until the next day, when we would come again.

The sun was still shining in the morning and we began to explore Whaddon Green. It seemed much smaller that I had remembered it. The road had been widened with the grass verge cut back, and the new trees, oaks and chestnuts, were set back from the highway, so that even when full-grown they would not be dangerous. The last of the elms stood all through the 'fifties; its loss grieved local people greatly. The first oak was planted by the then chairman of Wynstones teachers, Benedict Wood. Mr and Mrs Brunt, of Pound Farm, planted one special red oak. With all these trees, as yet only half-grown, there will be beauty once more in the years to come.

The little pond, of tragic memory, was still there, but the hedge surrounding it was so overgrown that we were only able to peer through it at the duckweed-covered water. Two walls of the old village pound remain. When I was very young, the pound was complete, and I remember once seeing a stray animal impounded there.

While my husband was obtaining permission to sketch Whaddon School, I telephoned friends and then walked along the Stroud road searching in vain for the Y.M.C.A. huts. A large school for senior children had been erected just below the spot where they had once stood. I asked the caretakers about the huts. They seemed to remember them vaguely as 'a little room where men of the football team once used to change'. The Money's house stood empty, their Mission Room had been sold. Two bungalows stand on the site of the Red Cross Room.

Near Whaddon Junior School (which is what my old school has turned into) the brook passes under the Stroud road. It disappears for a quarter of a mile. The road has been widened, so that only half of the old school garden remains. It was a green lawn when we saw it. The brook must run under the middle of the road now. The old thatched cottage has been replaced by a larger house of brick.

When my husband had finished drawing the school, we returned to the Green, where he began to sketch the pump which was still there, surrounded by high iron railings with a locked gate, just as I had always remembered it. Then, for the first time, I heard the story of the Well. For many years it provided water for the families living nearby but, as it was only 25 feet deep, it used to run dry when there were long periods without rain. Colonel Jeune tried to remedy this by having the well sunk to eighty feet. Alas! when it was refilled, the water was bitter and salt, as a mineral table had been breached in the process of drilling, and thus the well was rendered useless. Colonel Jeune decided that it would be best to fence it in with iron railing and keep the gate locked.

The story was told to us by Mr Charles Jones, who had been a pupil at Whaddon school when I was there. He also told us that a deeper well which served the Manor was still in use. It lies in fields between Tuffley and Whaddon and is reputed to be 120 feet deep. Water from it is pumped into a tank in the roof of the Manor, whence it was fed by gravity to the houses of workers on the estate. Most of the houses now have mains water, but the beautiful old Lister engine, which pumped the water many, many years ago, was still in perfect working order, its green paint with red and gold lettering as fresh as ever.

After an early lunch, we explored the area which was once our village. Rows and rows of houses spread out right to the boundary. These we approached through the old bridge, which had not altered much, though the road had been straightened. We searched for the Grange and eventually found it. Squeezed between smaller houses, its land all gone, it looks uncomfortable and apologetic. The straightened Grange Road has lost its meaning, now cut off from the house which gave it its name. Front gardens have been cut back, so that the old houses have an unbalanced appearance. Some of the older ones have vanished altogether. The farm which once stood opposite Whaddon School is no more; Whitcombe Farm and the Court itself are no longer visible. The farm which once stood opposite Whaddon School is no more. The Court and Tuffley Farm have both gone.

We sat talking to our friends for a time and then set out again for St. Margaret's church. We passed two aged perry pear trees, still standing on what was once the orchard of Tuffley Court. The New Inn has gone. Houses have been built up to the Stroud road and as far as the Whaddon boundary. The inhabitants of Whaddon feel that it is necessary to keep an ever-watchful eye on the activities of the City Corporation. What happened to Tuffley could very easily happen to them. Where our old village once stood, there is not a field left. It is now just a part of Gloucester.

St. Margaret's church was already unlocked for us and, as we entered, we found that in most ways it was as I remembered it. There were some changes: the shepherds' pews now hold a table top for books; the tortoise stove has been replaced by electric heaters; there are no choir stalls, for there is no choir today; the reed organ has been superseded by an electric one, after a long period in which a harmonium was used. The new organ is no longer situated in the chancel, but sits warmly beneath the still beautiful pulpit.

The Sinnott windows are as lovely as I remembered them and those at the East end, above the altar, still commemorate those who died in the wars. The old oak pews, each with its door to keep out draughts, are as warm and shining as ever. The brass eagle lectern and the vases and cross, which take hours of cleaning to keep them bright, are looked after by Alwyn Claridge, who was a fellow chorister of mine. There are newer tablets on the walls: one for those of the villagers who died in the Second World War, and another for James Sinnott, although he lived away from Tuffley, who had been killed at Halfaya Pass. On the door, a table of yearly costs set out the astronomical sum required to keep this small church alive. The few continue the struggle to meet them.

Returning to the Old Rectory, we met Mr and Mrs Vowles and we all talked with great excitement about this return journey. Sleep was not for me that night. I was not deeply sad but rather, in some inexplicable way, excited. So much had gone: fields, loved houses and places remembered. But everywhere there were flower-filled gardens; people were still as friendly and helpful as they had been in former times; so much had endured in a village which has become one of the largest in Gloucestershire.

Robert Browning surely encircled the meaning of life like a jewel in its setting when he wrote:

Earth changes, but thy soul and God stand sure;
What entered into thee
That was, is, and shall be,
Time's wheel runs back nor stops;
    Potter and Clay endure.